ELIZABETH BAGWELL FICKEN

that you may know the LORD

AN IN-DEPTH STUDY OF EZEKIEL

That You May Know The Lord © Copyright 2005,2010,2016
by Elizabeth Bagwell Ficken
Printed in the United States of America
First Printing, 2005
W & E Publishing, Cary, NC

Unless otherwise noted, Scripture quotations are from the Holy Bible,
New King James Version, copyright © 1979, 1980, 1982, Thomas Nelson, Inc.
Publishers. Used by permission. All rights reserved.

Scripture quotations identified NASB are from the
New American Standard Bible © The Lockman Foundation, 1960, 1962, 1963,
1968, 1971, 1972, 1973, 1975, 1977. Used by permission.

Scripture quotations identified NIV are from the *New International Version*,
copyright © 1973, 1978, 1984 by International Bible Society.

Scripture quotations identified NLT are from the Holy Bible,
New Living Translation, copyright © 1996. Used by permission of
Tyndale House Publisher, Inc., Wheaton, Illionois 60189. All rights reserved.

Scripture quotations identified The Message are from *THE MESSAGE*.
Copyright © by Eugene H. Peterson, 1993, 1994, 1995.
Used by permission of NavPress Publishing Group.

Scripture quotations identified KJV are from the *King James Version*.
"Do you know Jesus?" Gospel presentation from Sonlife Classic.
Copyright © 2009 Used by permission.

Front Cover: Michal Rudolph
Back Cover: Jeannine Klingbeil

Special thanks to:
My father, George Bagwell, who was the first person to teach me
about the dry bones, the Holy Spirit, and the book of Ezekiel;
and Paul Jackson (1955-2005), my pastor who encouraged
my study of Ezekiel, hermeneutics, and the Hebrew language.

"I will put My Spirit within you and cause you to walk in My statutes,
and you will keep My judgments and do them." Ezekiel 36:27

ISBN-10: 0-9905933-2-0
ISBN-13: 978-0-9905933-2-4

Table of Contents

Introduction   4
Do You Know Jesus?   5
Helpful Hints   6
My Bible Story   8

Unit 1   His Glorious Appearing
Ezekiel 1-3
- Lesson 1   The Word of the Lord   10
- Lesson 2   The Vision of the Lord   14
- Lesson 3   The Call of the Lord   19
- Lesson 4   The Requirement of the Lord   24

Unit 2   The Ominous Warning
Ezekiel 4-7
- Lesson 1   Fear and Famine   32
- Lesson 2   No Place to Hide   36
- Lesson 3   The Reason for it All   39
- Lesson 4   No Mercy   45

Unit 3   Travesty in the Temple
Ezekiel 8-11
- Lesson 1   Idols Adored   53
- Lesson 2   Wicked Slain   58
- Lesson 3   Glory Departs   63
- Lesson 4   Hope for the Hopeless   68

Unit 4   The Truth is Told
Ezekiel 12-14
- Lesson 1   Sign Language   77
- Lesson 2   Deceptive Declarations   81
- Lesson 3   False Forecasters   85
- Lesson 4   Hypocrites and Heroes   91

Unit 5   Powerful Parables
Ezekiel 15-17
- Lesson 1   The Worthless Vine   102
- Lesson 2   The Abandoned Baby   104
- Lesson 3   The Unfaithful Wife   111
- Lesson 4   The Withering Vine and the Majestic Cedar   114

Unit 6   Proclaiming the Prophecies
Ezekiel 18-21
- Lesson 1   Announcing Accountability   122
- Lesson 2   Lamenting the Leadership   125
- Lesson 3   Remembering the Past   128
- Lesson 4   Sounding the Alarm   132

Unit 7   The Refiner's Fire
Ezekiel 22-24
- Lesson 1   Bloodstained Hands   141
- Lesson 2   Sinful Sisters   145
- Lesson 3   The Final Judgment   148
- Lesson 4   Inexpressible Grief   151

Unit 8   Foreign Policies
Ezekiel 25-32
- Lesson 1   Nasty Neighbors   160
- Lesson 2   A Sinking Ship   165
- Lesson 3   Homeland Security   169
- Lesson 4   Pride and Punishment   174

Unit 9   A Change for the Better
Ezekiel 33-36
- Lesson 1   And It Came to Pass   181
- Lesson 2   A Prophet has been Among Them   183
- Lesson 3   The Best is Yet to Come   185
- Lesson 4   To the Mountains   191

Unit 10   Medical and Military Operations
Ezekiel 36-39
- Lesson 1   A Heart Transplant   198
- Lesson 2   Reconstructive Prophecy   201
- Lesson 3   National Unity   206
- Lesson 4   The Army of Gog   209

Unit 11   Great Expectations
Ezekiel 40-44
- Lesson 1   A Blueprint for Blessings   219
- Lesson 2   The Return of the Lord   223
- Lesson 3   Sacrifices to the Savior   226
- Lesson 4   Good and Faithful Servants   230

Unit 12   The Kingdom of Christ
Ezekiel 45-48
- Lesson 1   The Heart of Worship   238
- Lesson 2   The River of Life   244
- Lesson 3   The Covenant Fulfilled   247
- Lesson 4   The Lord is There   252

Endnotes   256
Suggested Resources   258
Other Studies by Elizabeth Bagwell Ficken   260

INTRODUCTION

Dear Friend,

When I was writing this study, I was asked how I chose Ezekiel for a Bible study. It would only be true to say that God chose Ezekiel for me. Years ago, I had a desire for my personal quiet times with the Lord grow in consistency and depth, so I determined to read a book of the Bible which I had not read before. The book of Ezekiel was unknown territory to me, and that's where I began.

I can clearly remember reading Chapter One and immediately turning to a commentary to try to understand the vision of the glory of the Lord. As I took in each aspect of Ezekiel's vision, I was amazed at the beauty of the Lord and His glory. I continued reading through the book on a daily basis.

I didn't understand everything that I read, but I kept noticing a repeated phrase – "that they may know the Lord" By the time I had finished reading the book, I still didn't really know what it was about, except that I had had a glimpse of the magnificent glory of the Lord, that Ezekiel was commanded to do some very strange things, that judgment predicted in the book was severe, and that the ultimate reason for all that God did was that "they may know the Lord."

The Lord used the book of Ezekiel in my life to prepare me to know Him in a new and exciting way. Seeing the glory of the Lord made me hunger to know Him more. I read Ezekiel a second time a year or so later. I'm sure I gleaned a little more understanding of the book at that time, but I don't remember anything in particular. And then, after a few more years had passed, once again I had the desire to read the book of Ezekiel during my quiet times. I just wanted to go slowly and see what the Lord would do. The first day, I didn't read past verse 1!

Three months later, I had completed my third time through the book of Ezekiel. And what a wonderful time it had been. Once again, I had been moved by the glory of the Lord. For the first time, I saw the obedient servant Ezekiel and was amazed at his faithfulness. I learned of the judgments of the Lord in a new way. I began to grasp a little bit of His future plans for Israel. He has unbelievable plans for His chosen nation! I realized that if the Lord can overcome the turmoil in the Middle East and make a place of peace and prosperity for Israel, then He certainly can overcome whatever turmoil may come into my life.

It is because of that third reading of the book of Ezekiel that I was moved to write a study on the book. I look back at the time that I decided to slowly read it for my quiet times. I have no idea why I chose Ezekiel at that point, but the book became familiar, and yet still intriguing territory. So here we are now, with an incredible journey of discovery ahead of us. I don't understand everything in this book of the Bible. It's full of unexplainable things. Even when we've completed our study, there will still be much more to learn. But this will be a precious time in the Scriptures and we will be taught by the Holy Spirit as He reveals truths to us so that "we may know the Lord."

DO YOU KNOW JESUS?

This is the most important question in this study. Please notice that I didn't ask you if you know about Jesus. But do you know Him, personally?

The Bible teaches that God loves you.
"For God so loved the world . . . that He gave His one and only son that whoever believes in Him will not perish, but have eternal life." John 3:16 ESV

And it teaches that God wants you to know Him personally.
"Now this is eternal life, that men may know Him, the only true God, and Jesus Christ whom He has sent." John 17:3 ESV

But . . . people are separated from God by their sin.
"Your sinful acts have alienated you from your God" Isaiah 59:2 NET

Sin causes us to miss the very best for our life.
"Jesus said, 'I came that you might have life and have it to the full." John 10:10 NIV

Sin causes us to face death and judgment.
"The wages of sin is death." Romans 3:32 NAS
"Those who do not know God . . . will pay the penalty of eternal destruction away from the presence of the Lord." 2 Thessalonians 1:8-9 NAS

But there is a solution! Jesus Christ died and conquered death for you! We deserve death and judgment, but Jesus took upon Himself the punishment for our sins, so that we could have a personal relationship with God.
"For there is only one God and one Mediator who can reconcile God and humanity-- the man Christ Jesus. He gave his life to purchase freedom for everyone." 1 Timothy 2:5-6 NLT

It's not enough just to know this. Each of us by faith must receive Jesus Christ if we want to know God personally.
"To all who have received Him—those who believe in His name—He has given the right to become God's children." John 1:12 NET
"For it is by grace you have been saved, through faith—and this not from yourselves, it is the gift of God." Ephesians 2:8 NIV

The ABC's of faith involve:
<u>Acknowledging your need</u>—admitting you have sinned and desiring to turn from sin. (1 John 1:8-9)
<u>Believing Jesus Christ died in your place</u> and rose again to be your Savior—providing forgiveness for your sins. (1 Corinthians 15:3-4:17)
<u>Choosing to invite Christ</u> to direct your life. (Romans 10:9)

Your desire to have a personal relationship with God can be expressed through a simple prayer like this: "Dear Lord, I want to know You personally. Thank you for sending Jesus who died in my place and rose again to be my Savior. Please forgive my sins. I am willing, with your help, to turn from my sins. Come into my life and lead me. Amen."

For illustrations and more information, go to **KnowHimPersonally.com**

HELPFUL HINTS

If you are new to in-depth Bible study. You will need a Bible. Please feel free to use the version of your choice. There are many translations. If you are using a Catholic Bible or a Jewish Old Testament it will be helpful for you to also use a modern version of the Bible which includes the Old and New Testament.

I recommend the following versions which are available for free at online Bible study websites, in smartphone and tablet apps (see recommendations on the next page), or for purchase in Christian bookstores. They are usually referred to by the letters in parentheses.

New King James Version (NKJV) New American Standard Version (NASB)
New International Version (NIV) Holman Christian Standard Bible (HCSB)
English Standard Version (ESV)

This study was written using multiple translations. I have found that I can gain understanding of the meaning of verses by reading other versions of the same passage. Two other popular Bibles are *The Message* and the New Living Translation (NLT); these are both wonderful versions for comparative reading, but are not as appropriate for in-depth study.

Planning time for your lesson. Set aside a specific amount of time to work on the lesson. One lesson may take 30-40 minutes depending on your familiarity with the Scriptures. You may want to do the lessons in shorter increments of time, depending on your schedule and personal preferences. I find that I absorb, retain, and apply the message of the Scriptures better when I am not rushed.

Please begin your study time with prayer. Ask the Holy Spirit to give you understanding of God's Word, as it is promised that He will do according to 1 Corinthians 2:12-13: "Now we have received, not the spirit of the world, but the Spirit who is from God, that we might know the things freely given to us by God, which things we also speak, not in words taught by human wisdom, but in those taught by the Spirit, combining spiritual thoughts with spiritual words." I have given you a reminder at the beginning of each lesson.

Observation, interpretation, and application. The Scripture readings, activities, cross-references and word definitions are all placed in the order which is most appropriate to your study. It is best to follow this order if you can, rather than skipping steps or setting steps aside to be completed at a different time. The order follows the inductive study process: observation (what the Scripture says), interpretation (what the author intended, what the Scripture means) and application (what difference the Scripture makes in your life). You will be doing the research, cross-referencing and summarization of the truths of each passage. When you finish a study of a passage, you will have gleaned more understanding on your own than you will find in some commentaries!

Looking up Hebrew word definitions. One of the activities included to help you understand the correct interpretation of the scripture is discovering and considering the definition of a word in its original language. Please make sure that you look up the definition of the word in its original language, not the definition of the English word. You will be given a prompt like this:

Meditate: Strong's #1897

Hebrew word:

Hebrew definition:

There are several ways you can look up the words given.
- You can google the Strong's reference number (Strong's 1897) and your web browser will give you links to the definition.
- You can go to an online Bible study website (recommendations below) and use their free reference materials. Look for "study" tabs, "lexicons" (this is what Hebrew and Greek word dictionaries are called), "concordances" and "original language" tools. There are search boxes where you can type in the Strong's reference number. Use H before the number for Hebrew words (H1897).

        studylight.org   blueletterbible.com   searchgodsword.org

Suggested resources, described on page 178, are also available at these websites if you want to do more research on your own.
- You can download free Bible study apps for your smartphone and/or tablet. I use **MySword** which allows me to go to a passage and click on the Strong's reference number next to the word. Try a few different ones and see what you like best.
- You may have some great resources on your own bookshelves! Enjoy using books like: *Strong's Exhaustive Concordance* and *The Complete Word Study Dictionary* by Spiros Zhodiates.

If you have trouble, it would be better to skip the exercise rather than filling in the English definition.

It's about your head and your heart. My hope is that you will read portions of Scripture and gain understanding of what is being communicated through them so that you can consider how to apply the truth of God's Word to your life. I have tried to make the study "user-friendly" and I promise that I don't ask trick questions. I do want to make you think hard sometimes though! I hope you won't get overwhelmed. Do what you can, a little bit at a time. The reward of knowing our holy God through His recorded word far outweighs the time and effort of study.

Prayer requests and praises. You will find pages at the end of each lesson which provide prompts from Scriptures for your prayers as well as a place for you to write out a personal prayer request . If you are studying with a group, it would be helpful to reflect on your personal prayer request before sharing it with the group. Keep your requests brief and personal. This page is also a place to record the prayer requests of others.

MY BIBLE STORY

I love my Bible! But I have about 10 of them on my bookshelf, so which one do I love and use to read and study? I'd like to answer that question with my Bible story.

The earliest Bible that I remember reading was a children's New Testament Living Bible. It was a birthday present from a friend when I was eight years old! I tried to read the book of Revelation, but didn't get very far. The next special Bible that I received was a black (faux) leather King James Version with Susan Elizabeth Bagwell engraved in gold letters on the front. This was from my parents, and it was my church Bible. I don't remember reading it at all, but I must have taken it to Sunday School with me because I found a Psalm 23 bookmark in it. That was to become the first well-known Scripture to me.

When I was fourteen I began using a paperback Bible which my father felt was an excellent translation. The New English Bible is not very well known, but it was the Bible that helped me begin to know God's Word. My Sunday school teacher actually made us read and study Ephesians so I began taking this Bible to church. I also underlined verses and took it with me to Bible studies in high school.

My first Bible with cross-references and helpful notes was the Ryrie Study Bible in the King James Version. A friend took me to the Baptist Bookstore, and I experienced picking out a Bible for myself. It was bound in dark blue leather and Elizabeth Bagwell was engraved in silver lettering. I bought it after high school graduation and used it for my quiet times and Bible study and sermon notes for about 10 years—through college and early marriage and the births of my children! It was falling apart and the bookbinder recommended a durable covering: blue canvas. I call it my blue jean Bible now!

Then I became aware of the New King James Version and decided it would be nice to leave behind the Thee's and Thou's of the Old King James . . . so I bought The Woman's Study Bible NJKV. It was refreshing to read God's truths in a new translation in a Bible that had clean pages where I could make new notes. Familiar verses were lovely and overlooked verses began to stand out as they had not done before. The changing of Bible translations became a new adventure for me.

I own and have read through the Bible in the NIV, NLT, NET, NAS, NKJ, ESV, and I'm currently reading through the HCSB. It is important to me to have a Bible with helpful study notes: historical and cultural information; word study definitions; maps; and appropriate cross-references. The layout of the Scriptures on the pages is important too! It just has to feel right! I have used the Archeological Study Bible and the Life Application Bible, but have enjoyed the Nelson Study Bible and the Holman Christian Standard Study Bible more.

Jesus loves me this I know, for my Bible tells me so! I love God's Word and I love my Bible—whichever one I may be reading at any given time.

UNIT ONE
His Glorious Appearing

LESSON ONE
The Word of the Lord
Background and Overview

LESSON TWO
The Vision of the Lord
EZEKIEL 1

LESSON THREE
The Call of the Lord
EZEKIEL 2 and 3

LESSON FOUR
The Requirement of the Lord
EZEKIEL 3

LESSON ONE — *The Word of the Lord* — EZEKIEL 1

Please pray for the Holy Spirit to give you an eagerness to understand the truth of the Word of God.

𐤉𐤄𐤅𐤄

A time machine. Traveling through the years. To the past, to the future, but always with the perspective of our present day. We are about to embark on a journey that will take us into the years before computers, satellites, iPhones, airplanes, and electricity. But the communication that we will see in the past is of the highest intelligence. The information communicated had no error, unlike our media today. The images we will see are more awesome than a 747 Jumbo Jet lifting off from a runway. And even without the special effects of computer design and engineering, these images will be fascinating.

We will go back in time before the birth of Christ, before the rise of the Roman Empire, before the rise and fall of the crusades of Alexander the Great. Our journey will begin 2,600 years before today. We will spend much of our time in the distant past, yet we will also travel to a time in the future – it could be as close as seven years from today. What we will see in the future will be a new world order which will last for one thousand years.

All you will need to take on this journey is a desire for truth and an attitude that is ready to respond to that truth. We will read, study, examine, and ponder the words of the Lord as spoken to Ezekiel, His priest turned prophet. Ready? We're going to set the dial for our first destination at 593 BC. Let's go!

Read Ezekiel 1:1-3.

How do we know that Ezekiel is the author of this book? What do you learn about him in these verses?

Where is Ezekiel when we first meet him? Research the location using a Bible dictionary, atlas, commentary – but don't read about anything past verse 3 yet! Record your findings.

What impression does this give you of Ezekiel's situation?

We're going to spend a lot of time looking at the dates that Ezekiel so carefully recorded. This may seem tedious, but in the end, it will actually present the whole context of the book of Ezekiel to you.

According to verse 1, when did Ezekiel hear from the Lord?

Numbers 4:1-3 sheds light on the signifigance and the most likely meaning of the "thirtieth year" mentioned in verse 1. What happened at that point in time? And what does that mean about Ezekiel?

That should explain the first set of dates mentioned, but then there is another set of dates to investigate. The historical and cultural setting of the book of Ezekiel will best be understood by studying the attacks on Israel by King Nebuchadnezzar of Babylon. There were three times when he attacked and took Israelites captive to Babylon.

The first is described most clearly in Daniel 1:1-7, the second in 2 Kings 24:8-17, and the third in 2 Kings 24:17-25:11. Study these passages, and fill in the chart below.

	King of Judah	**Year of attack**	**Taken captive or killed**
1st attack			
2nd attack			
3rd attack			

Although Ezekiel's name is not given in the description of those taken captive to Babylon with Jehoiachin, scholars have determined that the dates in his book give evidence that it was during that attack on Jerusalem that Ezekiel was taken to Babylon with the rest of his countrymen. The dates which Ezekiel gives us throughout his book are based on the number of years that he was in exile. Just as one trapped on a deserted island might count the days, months, and years that he is away from his home, so Ezekiel also based his "journal" on the number of years that he was away from his home in Israel.

Examine each of the following verses in which Ezekiel records the exact date that the Lord spoke to Him. Record the timing as he did: year of captivity, day, month, location, and topic if that is easily noted.

And the word of the Lord came to Ezekiel...

Verse	Year of captivity	Month	Day of month	Location, topic
Ezekiel 1:1-2				
Ezekiel 8:1				
Ezekiel 20:1				
Ezekiel 24:1-2				
Ezekiel 26:1-2				
Ezekiel 29:1-2				
Ezekiel 29:17				
Ezekiel 30:20				
Ezekiel 31:1				
Ezekiel 32:1-2				
Ezekiel 32:17				
Ezekiel 33:21				
Ezekiel 40:1-2				

Five years after Jehoiachin was taken captive, Ezekiel states that he received the word of the Lord. The journal entries we just looked at cover about 20 years of time.

What do you notice about the Lord's timing of communicating with Ezekiel?

Does this have any impact on your understanding of the Lord's timing in speaking to you?

Congratulations! You have just traveled from the present back to 605 BC when the first Israelites (Daniel and friends) were taken captive by Nebuchadnezzar, King of Babylon. Then time marched on, although slowly and painfully for Ezekiel and the exiles. Ezekiel recorded his role as prophet, which spanned 20 years, but his visions spanned several millennia!

The circumstances in which Ezekiel found himself were heartbreaking. He had been preparing to serve the Lord as a priest in the temple which had been built by Solomon. As we will see in future studies, he was devoted to the Lord and had kept himself pure. Now he was a stranger in a pagan country. Exiled. Grieving. Waiting. But in the darkest period of Ezekiel's life, the Lord was going to come to him in all of His glory.

What are your circumstances today? Do you long to see the Lord? Close today's study with a prayer expressing your desire for Him.

Blessed are those who see the hand of God in the haphazard, inexplicable, and seemingly senseless circumstances of life.[1] ERWIN W. LUTZER (1941–)

LESSON TWO *The Vision of the Lord* **EZEKIEL 1**

Pray that the God of our Lord Jesus Christ, the Father of glory, would give to you the spirit of wisdom and revelation, that the eyes of your understanding would be enlightened, and that you would know the hope of His calling.

𐤉𐤄𐤅𐤄

Prepare to see the glory of the Lord as revealed to Ezekiel.

Slowly read Ezekiel Chapter 1. The fear of the Lord is the beginning of wisdom. Just read the text, without consulting commentaries at this point.

What "came to pass" in verse 1?

What phrases in verse 3 indicate that Ezekiel experienced something outside of his ordinary routine?

The phrase "the word of the Lord" is used over 60 times throughout this book. Plan on marking, highlighting, or underlining it each time you see it. The Word of the Lord did not come to everyone in those days. The people wanted to hear from Him, but they didn't always want to hear what He had to say to them. A time would come when the Lord would be silent – for four hundred years. And then, in the fullness of time, the Word of the Lord came again. "And the Word became flesh and dwelt among us, and we beheld His glory, the glory as of the only begotten of the Father, full of grace and truth."

Please remember that you can always hear the Word of the Lord when you open your Bible. The Lord is there.

Using terms from Scripture, in order of appearance, describe what Ezekiel saw in verses 4-25.

What do the repeated terms "appearance" and "likeness" imply to you? Why do you think they were used over and over?

Look at the following Scriptures and compare Ezekiel's vision with these other manifestations and visions of the Lord. Note the similarities, the symbolism or purpose if given, and the differences.

Jeremiah 23:18-20

Exodus 19:16-20

Psalm 18:6-14

Isaiah 6:1-8

Revelation 4:2-9

Jump ahead for a moment to Ezekiel 10, reading the chapter in its entirety, to see another description by Ezekiel about the living creatures. Note any further explanation, description or actions regarding the living creatures.

Let's look at a few other Scriptures which mention cherub (singular) or cherubim (plural). Where do you find them? What are their purposes?

Genesis 3:24

Exodus 25:17-20

Exodus 26:31

Pause and reflect on the honor and obedience that these creatures give to the Lord. Did you know that angels "desire to look into" the gospel and they don't receive salvation from Jesus Christ? Do you think that you have more for which to give honor and obedience and glory to the Lord than they do? Should the cherubim "out-praise" you?

While the images of the whirlwind, cherubim, and wheels are fascinating, they pale in comparison to Who Ezekiel saw above the chariot, above the "firmament." List as many details as you can from Ezekiel 1:26-28.

"This was the appearance of the likeness of the glory of the Lord." Ezekiel 1:28

Please look up the meaning for:
Glory: Strong's #3519
Hebrew word:
Hebrew definition:

Who is this? Turn to Hebrews 1:1-4 to discover the answer; make sure you notice the word "glory." Record what you learn.

There are so many people who want to see God. He has already shown Himself and is still able to be seen everyday! I mentioned yesterday that all you needed for this journey was a desire for the truth and an attitude willing to respond to the truth. The Scripture that we hold in our hands is the truth. What you read in black and white is reality.

Look at the following references to continue to see the Lord. Make notes of what you see.

Exodus 24:9-11

Joshua 5:13-15

Daniel 10:4-7

Luke 9:28-36

Revelation 1:12-18

The vision of the glory of the Lord was the preparation for Ezekiel to be the servant of the Lord. In this awesome, unexplainable encounter, Ezekiel saw the Lord for Who He is: Holy, Supernatural, Above All, a Consuming Fire.

What was Ezekiel's response?

Another man saw the Lord and responded in the same way. Look at the following passage, noting the similarities in the vision, and then note the instructions given.

Acts 26:12-18

Have you seen the glory of the Lord? Do you know Him? 2 Corinthians 4:6 says "For it is God who commanded light to shine out of darkness, who has shone in our hearts to give the light of the knowledge of the glory of God in the face of Jesus Christ." You will only be able to see God if you have seen Jesus. Ezekiel knew who God was and had been preparing to be His priest, but he had not personally experienced Him. The apostle Paul was a religious leader and knew who God was, but he had rejected Jesus. When these two men saw the Lord in His glory they were never the same again.

How do you respond to the vision of the glory of the Lord today?

LESSON THREE   *The Call of the Lord*   EZEKIEL 2 and 3

Pray that the Holy Spirit will give you understanding of the call to be a servant.

ヨYヨV

Today, we will see what happens after a man encounters the glorious Lord. Ezekiel's response will challenge and inspire us.

A Christian servant is one who perpetually looks into the face of God and then goes forth to talk to others. [2]   Oswald Chambers

---

I'm going to ask you to read Chapter 1 again, continuing through until Ezekiel 3:16. Throughout this study, I will ask you to reread passages and chapters so that the images and messages in this book will become more familiar. At your first readings, the signs, parables, and visions will be bizarre, outlandish, and extraordinary. As they become more familiar you will gain a better understanding of the Lord and His message, and of Ezekiel and his mission.

Please read Ezekiel 1:1 - 3:16.

In the previous lesson, we observed that Ezekiel's immediate reaction to seeing the glory of the Lord was to fall on his face. He humbled himself before his awesome and holy God. What happened next? Look for who, what, and how in Ezekiel 1:28 — 2:2. Record what you learn.

*Ezekiel's initial encounter with the Lord was primarily visual as he **saw** the glory of the Lord. This prepared him to **hear** the Lord and receive his commission from the Lord. For the next 20 years the word of the Lord will be spoken to Ezekiel. He will hear it and speak what he hears.*

Study Ezekiel 2:1 — 3:11 and list on the chart on the next page each of the instructions given to Ezekiel (even those repeated) and then list the description of Israel (include all repetitions).

Instructions to Ezekiel	Descriptions of Israel

What are your first impressions of the Lord's commission to Ezekiel?

What do you think about the way the Lord described His chosen people, the nation of Israel?

Do you personally relate to anything we've observed so far? Do you have clear instructions from the Lord regarding some service to Him? Do you have a call that seems that it will be extremely difficult? Are you being led to live as an obedient servant of the Lord among rebellious, stubborn, or hard-hearted people? Are you perhaps a rebellious child, not listening to what the Lord is saying to you?

Spend a few moments responding to the Lord in whatever way is personally appropriate for you at this time.

The commission of Ezekiel did not come without a commitment from the Lord. Read the following verses and note how Ezekiel was enabled to obey.

Ezekiel 2:2

Ezekiel 2:9-3:3

Ezekiel 3:8-10

Ezekiel 3:12-14

Please look up the meaning for the following word:
Adamant: Strong's #8068
Hebrew word:
Hebrew definition:

Even though the house of Israel was rebellious and hard-hearted, Ezekiel was given hard-headedness! There is diamond-like beauty in being adamant about the truth of the Lord.

There are a few more words and phrases whose meanings will add to our understanding of Ezekiel's commission and the Lord's commitment to him.

Please look up the meaning for:
Bitterness: Strong's #4751
Hebrew word:
Hebrew definition:

Heat: Strong's #2534
Hebrew word:
Hebrew definition:

Astonished: Strong's #8074
Hebrew word:
Hebrew definition:

Now read Ezekiel 3:15 and note where Ezekiel was placed, who he was with, and what he did.

Based on the definition of the words you looked up, look again at Ezekiel 3:14,15 and describe in your own words Ezekiel's reaction to his new assignment.

"But the hand of the Lord was strong upon me. . ." Despite the extreme grief from being in captivity, despite the overwhelming responsibility to announce the coming judgment of God, despite the personal anguish which Ezekiel felt, the hand of the Lord was strong enough to sustain him and empower him to obey. He would experience this strength throughout the duration of his ministry.

Look at the following verses and note the circumstance in which Ezekiel finds himself and what happens when the hand of the Lord comes upon him.

Ezekiel 3:14

Ezekiel 3:22

Ezekiel 8:1

Ezekiel 33:22, 23

Ezekiel 37:1

Equal in importance to the hand of the Lord was the enabling of the Holy Spirit. Look at the following verses and note what the Spirit does.

Ezekiel 2:2

Ezekiel 3:12, 14

Ezekiel 3:23, 24

Ezekiel 8:3

Ezekiel 11:1, 5, 24

Ezekiel 43:5

In the Old Testament, God selectively empowered those whom He chose for service to Him. The Scriptures record the times that the Spirit of the Lord came upon men such as Gideon, Samson, Saul and David. The Lord isn't looking for a few good men. He is looking for one receptive man or woman. The men just listed are examples of weakness, timidity, lustfulness, pride, and youth. The Lord has His reasons for choosing common, pathetic people!

Look at the following references and note the Lord's desire.

Zechariah 4:6

2 Corinthians 4:7

2 Corinthians 12:9, 10

As we close this lesson today, consider again the instructions given to Ezekiel. Perhaps you found yourself identifying with him because of some situation which you are facing, whether it be a trial or an opportunity for ministry. If you have seen Jesus face-to-face and accepted Him as your Savior, then the Holy Spirit has already come upon you, as He came upon Ezekiel, to strengthen you and equip you to follow the Lord. Jesus spoke His final promise from the Mount of Olives before ascending into heaven. He prepared the disciples for their new assignment, and His words to them are for you as well.

"You shall receive power when the Holy Spirit has come upon you; and you shall be witnesses to Me in Jerusalem, and in all Judea and Samaria, and to the end of the earth." Acts 1:8

What are you doing in the power of the Spirit? How is the hand of the Lord strengthening you today?

LESSON FOUR — *The Requirement of the Lord* — EZEKIEL 3

Pray that as we study we will heed the warnings and understand the signs.

יהוה

Please begin your study today by starting your reading at Ezekiel 2 and continuing through the end of Chapter 3. You will see Ezekiel as a watchman with a warning, as a shut-in at home, and as a servant made silent. After reading Ezekiel 2 – 3 please look up the following words:

Watchman: Strong's #6822

Hebrew word:

Hebrew definition:

Warning: Strong's #2094

Hebrew word:

Hebrew definition:

If you have a watchdog at home, then you can easily imagine the role of a watchman on the walls of the ancient cities. When something out of the ordinary is approaching, doesn't a watchdog sound his alarm, with excited barking? That was the basic idea for the watchmen way back then. If the watchman did not sound an alarm, and the city was attacked, the watchman would be held accountable. If people within the city were killed, then the watchman would be the one guilty of their death.

What was the warning that the Lord gave to Ezekiel? Please list the four different scenarios described in Ezekiel 3:17-21.

If you were Ezekiel, which of the scenarios above would you want to see take place? Which is the worst-case scenario, and which is the best-case scenario?

The call to be a watchman is repeated to Ezekiel in Chapter 33. Turn there and read Ezekiel 33: 1-11. Note the scenarios described and what the Lord ultimately desires.

In today's culture, we have been given watchmen who speak warnings to us as well. Our church leaders have the same serious responsibility that was given to Ezekiel. Turn to Hebrews 13:7, 17. What is their responsibility, and what is your responsibility?

We are to pay attention to the warnings sounded by the watchmen that the Lord places in our lives. They may come in the form of friends or family, teachers or pastors, or the warning may come straight from the Word of God.

Consider again the desire of the Lord as seen in Ezekiel 33:11. He takes no pleasure in the death of the wicked but wants them to turn from their sin. Is the Lord calling you to be a watchman, sounding a warning to those around you who are without Christ, leading them to repentance and forgiveness and life? Take a moment and allow the Lord to impress upon you His instructions for you right now.

What an overwhelming, awesome responsibility. "His blood I will require at your hand." If I were Ezekiel, I would certainly want to make sure that I sounded every warning that the Lord gave me. But I think that I would be afraid of my own inadequacy for such a calling. It was the perfect timing for the Lord to lay His hand upon Ezekiel again.

What happens in Ezekiel 3:22-23, and why do you think it happens?

What new instructions and information does Ezekiel receive from the Spirit in Ezekiel 3:24-27?

What, if anything, surprises you about the Lord's plan that you've just looked at?

Various commentaries indicate that the Lord chose to shut Ezekiel in his own house because He knew that the Israelites were not going to listen to him. They might even attack him thinking that he was a madman. But from his own house Ezekiel could preach sermons and the people would come observe him, then ask him what he was doing.

The rebellious house of Israel had already turned a deaf ear on the Words of the Lord spoken to them by other prophets. Now the Lord places a prophet in their midst with His Words again, but keeps him silent. The lesson for us today is: don't take the Word of God for granted.

It's only the beginning of Ezekiel's life as a visual display of the messages of the Lord. Things are going to get pretty strange around Ezekiel's house. We are never formally introduced to the "Mrs.," but she is there. Today's scholars are asking if Ezekiel was mentally unbalanced. Imagine what the neighbors thought!

Just to give you a glimpse of the weird and wonderful sermons to be preached by Ezekiel, look ahead at the following verses and briefly summarize what the Lord instructs him to do. Just the facts for now, we'll look at the purpose of these sermons as we come to them!

Ezekiel 4:4-6

Ezekiel 5:1-2

Ezekiel 12:7

Ezekiel 12:17-18

Ezekiel 24:15-18

How would you like to go to Ezekiel's church? His messages are never dull and boring! I hope you are intrigued by what you've had a glimpse of. Ezekiel obeyed the Lord in every case. He was a faithful watchman, sounding out all the warnings given to him by the Lord and he was not held responsible for the rebelliousness of the house of Israel.

We have clear instructions from the Lord on how to follow Him. What do you see in the following verses that Ezekiel obviously understood in his heart before these words were ever spoken?

Luke 9:23

Philippians 3:7-9

Please reflect now on the vision of the glory of the Lord seen in Ezekiel 1. Read this chapter again. How does this vision set the stage for the call of Ezekiel and the message that he must deliver?

> God was able to work in Ezekiel so mightily because he was pliable and instantly obedient to the Holy Spirit of God. See throughout the story, from this chapter onwards, not the smallest resistance to the revealed will of God or hesitation in obedience. God could count on him to fulfill His will. What a blessed picture of the surrendered life! How few of us are willing for this utter surrender, this absolute abandonment. It can only be upon these conditions – all private interests and personal considerations utterly merged in the interests of God and of His kingdom.[3]

Complete surrender to the Lord. Loving the Lord with all of our heart, soul, mind and strength enables us to let go of the other things we love or think we need. What we receive in return will be the great reward of the Lord Himself. Just ask Ezekiel. Do you think he would have traded his vision of the glory of the Lord for anything? Are you willing to absolutely abandon yourself to the Lord, no matter what the cost? Close this week's study with prayer and reflection on this.

Reviewing the Revelations

Unit One

His Glorious Appearing

Ezekiel 1-3

◈ What were the most meaningful Scriptures or truths from this unit's lessons?

◈ How do these truths impact your daily life?

◈ Is there anything that you have questions about?

Prayer Requests and Praises

Today's Date:

My personal request:

Confidential requests from my friends:

...Far be it from me that I should sin against You, O Lord, by ceasing to pray for others.

1 Samuel 12:23

Notes

UNIT TWO

The Ominous Warning

LESSON ONE
Fear and Famine
EZEKIEL 4

LESSON TWO
No Place to Hide
EZEKIEL 5

LESSON THREE
The Reason for It All
EZEKIEL 6

LESSON FOUR
No Mercy
EZEKIEL 7

LESSON ONE   *Fear and Famine*   EZEKIEL 4

Pray that the Holy Spirit will lead you to see that "all Scripture is profitable for doctrine, for reproof, for correction, and for instruction..." that we may be thoroughly equipped for every good work.

יהוה

This week we will begin our study of the lamentations, mournings, and woes that Ezekiel saw in the scroll which he was given to eat. Chapters 4 – 32 are about the Lord's judgment against Israel as well as against Gentile nations such as Egypt and Babylon. Please remember that Ezekiel accepted the scroll from the Lord and ate it. He took it into his belly, and received it into his heart, and heard it with his ears. (Ezekiel 3:3,10) The words were like honey to him because they were from the Lord, but they caused him great distress because of their truths.

We are to hear the Word of the Lord, and receive His truth into our hearts. Let's look at a message given to Christians in the early church to prepare our hearts.

Read Hebrews 3:7-19.

How did the Israelites respond to the Lord in the wilderness?

What warning is being given to believers "today?"

"So we see that they could not enter in because of their _____" Hebrews 3:19

Unbelief is the root of disobedience. We are creatures with a bent toward selfishness, but it is unbelief that opens the door to act out in self-centeredness which is disobedience, or rebellion. Christians might not think that they sin because of unbelief. But unbelief shows up in the life of a Christian when she does not respond to the Lord as Who He says He is, and when she does not respond to His Word as the Truth. Ezekiel has just seen the glory of the Lord and believes that He is Who He says He is. You will see over and over again in this book that the Lord speaks His messages and judgments so that "they shall know that I am the Lord."

Please read Ezekiel 3:22 – 4:17.

What is your reaction to the instructions given to Ezekiel in Chapter 4?

What was Ezekiel's reaction? This is one of the few comments made by Ezekiel that gives us insight into his character. What do you learn about him from Ezekiel 4:14?

Look at Leviticus 22:1, 2, 8 and note the instructions given for priests.

Despite the hundreds of years of wickedness even among priests, Ezekiel had followed the Word of God given by Moses.

Describe from the verses below the actions which Ezekiel was to perform.

Ezekiel 4:1-3

Ezekiel 4:4-5

Ezekiel 4:6-7

Ezekiel 4:9-12, 15

Read through Ezekiel 4 again and record the Lord's purposes or explanations for the actions which He required Ezekiel to take.

Keeping with his call to be a watchman, Ezekiel is also named as a sign to the house of Israel. Record what the Lord says in the following verses.

Ezekiel 12:6

Ezekiel 12:11

Ezekiel 24:24

Ezekiel 24:27

According to Ezekiel 1:2, these actions in Ezekiel 4 occurred during the fifth year of the captivity of Jehoiachin, King of Judah. This was in 597 BC.

Turn to 2 Kings 25:1-3 and record what happened and when it happened. Calculate the year of this occurrence using 597 BC as the first year of the reign of King Zedekiah. Remember that before Christ, the years count down to zero. (You have to subtract!)

What does this indicate to you regarding Ezekiel's actions in Chapter 4? How far in advance did the Lord warn of the judgment to come to people of Jerusalem? How accurate was the portrayal of the judgment?

Because we can look back at history from the present day perspective, we can see that the Word of the Lord was fulfilled in its entirety regarding the siege of Jerusalem. While Ezekiel and his fellow captives would have to wait nine years before seeing the judgment carried out, we don't have to wait at all to see that what the Lord spoke came to pass. Let this serve as a starting point for us to hear the Word of the Lord and believe it. What we will study in Ezekiel either has been fulfilled or will be fulfilled.

A historian is a prophet in reverse.[1]

AUGUST WILHELM VON SCHLEGEL (1767–1845)

Throughout the book of Ezekiel, the Lord makes it clear to the prophet that the house of Israel had been a rebellious nation from the time that the Lord made them His chosen people. You have just seen that Ezekiel would demonstrate their sin by lying on his side for the number of days equal to their years of iniquity. Commentators have various explanations for why the Lord chose the numbers 390 and 40. What makes the most sense to me is that there were approximately 390 years of a divided kingdom, in which the Northern Kingdom of Israel rebelled against the Lord and His covenant. There were 40 years of rebellion from the children of Israel in the wilderness after their exodus from Egypt. God's chosen people had been strong-willed, stiff-necked, self-centered sinners for their entire existence.

Read 2 Kings 17: 7 – 20 and record the sins committed by the children of Israel.

Do you remember the description of the house of Israel from last week's study? Turn back to it for just a moment – page 20. What do you think about the Lord's assessment of His people?

Summarize what you learn about the Lord from the following verses:

2 Kings 13:23 (around 800 BC)

2 Kings 24:18-20 (586 BC)

Isaiah 55:6-7 (around 700 BC)

Ezekiel 18:30-32 (592 BC)

Acts 3:18-19 (around AD 30-35)

2 Peter 3:9 (around AD 64 – 67)

I once heard that we should be able to turn to any passage in the Bible and let it point us to Jesus. The Lord has certainly led us that way today.

Acts 2:36 – 39: "Therefore let all the house of Israel know assuredly, that God hath made that same Jesus, whom ye have crucified, both Lord and Christ. Now when they heard this, they were pricked in their heart, and said unto Peter and to the rest of the apostles, Men and brethren, what shall we do? Then Peter said unto them, Repent, and be baptized every one of you in the name of Jesus Christ for the remission of sins, and ye shall receive the gift of the Holy Ghost. For the promise is unto you, and to your children, and to all that are afar off, even as many as the Lord our God shall call."

Jesus is the one who offers forgiveness and life. It doesn't matter what your sin is; you can be forgiven. Are you turning aside from the ways of the Lord? Look over the list of the sins of Israel from 2 Kings. Have you modernized any of their acts of disobedience? Are you rationalizing any unbelief? The Word of God is a warning to us. For the righteous, to continue in righteousness. For the sinner, to turn from his rebellious ways.

I exhort you today dear friend, lest any of you be hardened by the deceitfulness of sin. Turn to the Lord. If you are "pricked in your heart," then repent of your sin and be forgiven. If you are walking in righteousness, then pray for continued faithfulness.

LESSON TWO — No Place to Hide — EZEKIEL 5

Pray for a love of the Word of God and a whole-hearted love of the God of the Word.

יהוה

Please read Ezekiel 4:1 – 5:17.

What does the Lord instruct Ezekiel to do now regarding the visual display of the siege of Jerusalem which was set up in Chapter 4?

The command in Ezekiel 5:1 must have come as a shock to Ezekiel who had been preparing all of his life to be a priest. Look at another one of the rules of conduct for the priesthood in Leviticus 21:5, 6. What were they not to do and why?

Have you ever received instructions from the Lord that seem to go against common sense or even "Christian sense"? If so, what were they and how did you respond?

The Lord explains the meanings and the reasons for His instructions very clearly in Chapter 5. In the chart on the next page, list the specific actions of Ezekiel from verses 2-4, and then list the meanings of these actions given in verse 12.

Ezekiel's Actions: Ezekiel 5:2	The Lord's Explanation: Ezekiel 5:12

Remember that we learned yesterday that through Ezekiel in 597 BC, the Lord was warning the house of Israel of the siege that would come to Jerusalem in 586 BC.

Turn to the following verses and record how the Word of God was fulfilled.

2 Kings 25:8-12

2 Kings 25:18-21

Read Ezekiel 5:1-11 again and this time list the reasons the Lord gives for the judgments He planned to execute against the house of Israel.

"This is _____; I have set her in the midst of the nations and the countries all around her." Ezekiel 5:5

What is this city to be? Record what you find in Psalm 48:2 and Psalm 135:21.

And what was the nation of Israel to do and be according to Deuteronomy 28:1-2?

> God's people and city actually stand in the central point of the God-directed world-development and its movements.[2]

What would be their consequences for disobeying the commandments of the Lord? Record your answers from the following verses.

Deuteronomy 28:15

Deuteronomy 28:20-22

Deuteronomy 28:36-37

Deuteronomy 28:52-53

Deuteronomy 28:64-65

Was the Lord right to bring about judgments against the house of Israel? Why or why not?

The Lord spoke to the house of Israel with passion and zeal. What strong words did He say to them in Ezekiel 5:8, 9 and 13?

The Lord executed judgment against Israel because they had sinned against Him. What would be the result of this according to Ezekiel 5:14-15?

Isaiah 26:9 says, "When Your judgments are in the earth, the inhabitants of the world will learn righteousness." What does Jeremiah 22:8, 9 say?

What does Jesus say? Turn to Matthew 5:16 and record your answer.

What lessons can you learn from the house of Israel today? Think about who they were chosen to be and how they behaved. Who are you and what is required of you? The first commandment given to the Israelites is still the greatest commandment of all. Write out and personalize Mark 12:30.

LESSON THREE *The Reason for it All* **EZEKIEL 6**

Pray that you will rejoice when the Word of the Lord is spoken to you.

יהוה

The theme of Ezekiel 6 in my Bible is "Judgment on Idolatrous Israel." After the past two days' lessons on the sin and judgment of Israel, that probably doesn't sound too exciting to you right now. But I am looking forward to studying this chapter. It has a hint of hope and it has the first occurrence of the ultimate result of the judgment on Israel. Are you a little more excited now? You'll need to plan a little more time for this lesson—it has 2 sections.

Please read Ezekiel 6:1-14.

Before we consider the hope which I mentioned, and before we look at the ultimate result of the judgment on Israel, we have to look at the specifics of this particular Word of the Lord.

List the various places that the prophecy in Ezekiel 6 is against, including the areas where the people lie slain.

Using a Bible dictionary or Bible encyclopedia, look up "high places" and "idols" and record what you learn about them.

What were the Israelites to do in the Promised Land according to Numbers 33:52?

What did they do instead? Record your answer from 1 Kings 14:23 and 2 Kings 17:9-11.

What will be destroyed according to Ezekiel 6:3-6?

The Lord spoke to Moses in the wilderness to prepare the Israelites for their life in the Promised Land. Turn to Leviticus and record His Words from the following verses.

Leviticus 26:1

Leviticus 26:27-33

Did you notice that Ezekiel 6:5 and Leviticus 26:30 are identical? The Lord is the same, yesterday, today, and tomorrow.

Was it just the Israelites of ancient times that had a problem with idolatry? No, the first Christians were exhorted to beware of this sin against the Lord as well. Idolatry takes on many different forms. What do you learn from Colossians 3:1-5?

The "high places" that we are to spend our time and affection on are those things that are above – where Christ is seated at the right hand of God. That's a high place worth worshipping! Spend a few moments there in His presence now, offering sweet incense to Him in the form of prayer and praise.

The Lord God Omnipotent Reigns! And He is faithful to His Word. What hope does He give to the captives in Ezekiel 6:8, 9?

Compare this with the Word of the Lord in Leviticus 26:44-45 and Deuteronomy 4:25-31. What will the Lord remember? What warning was given? How would the people respond? What do you learn about the Lord from these verses?

SECTION 2

Please read Ezekiel 6:1-14 again.

When the Word of the Lord comes to Ezekiel in Chapter 6, it is the first time since his commission as a prophet that he is actually given words to speak to the exiles. Up until this point, his "sermons" have been intriguing visual demonstrations!

Who the message is from is obvious to us, but was also unmistakable for the exiles. Record exactly what Ezekiel is told to say regarding the author of this prophesy. See Ezekiel 6:3 and 6:11.

Highlight, circle, or underline the ultimate result of the judgment of the house of Israel. It's the key phrase which will be repeated throughout the book of Ezekiel. You'll find it four times in Ezekiel 6. What is it?

Perhaps you've noticed different typesetting such as "Lord," "LORD," and "GOD." In Ezekiel 6:1, 3, 7 and throughout the whole book, different names for the Lord are used. We are going to do some research on these names of the Lord. As you contemplate what you learn, keep in mind the context of this chapter. The house of Israel is being judged because of their worship of false gods and idols.

Look up the definitions for the following words. You may find it helpful to also look in a Bible dictionary or Bible encyclopedia for further explanations.

LORD: Strong's #3068 (Ezekiel 6:1)

Ancient Hebrew word: 𐤉𐤄𐤅𐤄

Hebrew word:

Hebrew definition:

Lord: Strong's #136 (Ezekiel 6:3)

Hebrew word:

Hebrew definition:

GOD: Strong's #3069 (Ezekiel 6:3)

Hebrew word:

Hebrew definition:

God: Strong's #430 (Exodus 3:14)

Hebrew word:

Hebrew definition:

Summarize your findings and explain the difference in these names of God.

Let's look at the time the Lord first introduced Himself and gave His name. In Exodus 6:3 the Lord says, "I appeared to Abraham, to Isaac and to Jacob as God Almighty, but by My name the Lord I did not make Myself known to them." Turn to Exodus 3:1 and remember that you are in the presence of the living holy God.

Read Exodus 3:1-6. How does the Lord show His Holiness in this meeting with Moses?

Read Exodus 3:13-15. What do you learn about the name of the Lord in these verses?

*The name **Yahweh** (LORD—Strong's #3068) has as its root word, **hayah** (Strong's #1961) which means "to exist, to be" and is translated in Exodus 3:14 as "I AM." As you can see in Ezekiel 6:7 below and perhaps in your own Bible, the word "am" is in italics. This indicates that the expression in the original language required clarification through additional English words. What the Lord was saying through Ezekiel to all the house of Israel was "you will know that I AM THAT I AM." The Lord was keeping His covenant with His chosen people. He had promised them from the beginning that they would know that He is the Lord. Exodus 6:7 says: "I will take you as My people, and I will be your God. Then you shall know that I am the Lord your God who brings you out from under the burdens of the Egyptians."*

Using different colors highlight each of the names of God in the verses below. Write the Hebrew word for each name above the English word. Refer to your Hebrew words and definitions on the previous page.

Exodus 3:14 And God[430] said[559] unto[413] Moses,[4872] I AM[1961] THAT[834] I AM:[1961] and he said,[559] Thus[3541] shalt thou say[559] unto the children[1121] of Israel,[3478] I AM[1961] hath sent[7971] me unto[413] you.

Ezekiel 6:1 And the word[1697] of the LORD[3068] came[1961] unto[413] me...

Ezekiel 6:3 And say,[559] Ye mountains[2022] of Israel,[3478] hear[8085] the word[1697] of the Lord[136] GOD;[3069] Thus[3541] saith[559] the Lord[136] GOD[3069]

Ezekiel 6:7 and ye shall know[3045] that[3588] I *am* the LORD.[3068]

Now for a few statistics and then we'll draw some conclusions.

English (Strong's #)	Hebrew	Meaning	Number of times used in Ezekiel
LORD (3068)	*YHWH*	I AM THAT I AM	217
GOD (3069)	*Jehovah*	The Self-existent One	217
God (430)	*Elohim*	Supreme God, Creator	36
Lord (136)	*Adonai*	Lord, Master	222

The Name of the Lord is mentioned 692 times in Ezekiel's 48 chapters and 1263 verses. And in the very last verse of the book, the Lord announces a new name for Himself: YHWH SHAMMAH – THE LORD IS THERE. The LORD is there, all the time, speaking, with the desire that the house of Israel know Him.

There is one more point that I came across in my research of the names of the Lord:

> The name Yahweh is used when the Bible wishes to present the personal character of God and his direct relationship with those human beings who have a special association with him. Contrariwise, Elohim occurs when the Scriptures are referring to God as a transcendent Being who is the author of the material world, yet One who stands above it. [3]

Look at the chart on the previous page which lists the number of times the different names of the Lord are used. Look at the number of times that Elohim is used, compared to the number of times that YHWH is used. What does this indicate to you that the Lord wanted to communicate to the exiles?

Our study on the names of the Lord would not be complete without looking at the most beautiful name of all. Please turn to Philippians 2:9-11. Note everything that you can learn about the name described in these verses.

Look back at the beginning of this lesson to recall the specific reasons the Lord gave for the judgment He would carry out on the house of Israel. Do you think Philippians 2:9-11 is applicable here? If so, how?

The Lord introduced Himself to Moses thousands of years ago and announced His Holy Name. Jesus introduced Himself to people over a three year period of time and announced many names by which He could be known. Which of the names of Jesus are most personal and meaningful to you? Close your study time today exalting the name of Jesus, giving Him the highest place of honor and worship in your life.

LESSON FOUR   *No Mercy*   EZEKIEL 7

Pray that the Holy Spirit would give you understanding of the Word of the Lord today.

יהוה

Today we will look at the last Word of the Lord given to Ezekiel during his very first year as a prophet. He is still in his home, and probably still in the process of lying on his left side and eating his rationed bread and water. He was counting down until the 390th day of the demonstration of the sin of Israel was completed.

The first words from the Lord in Ezekiel 7:2, 3 are: "An end! The end has come....Now the end has come upon you." We might think that the excitement was because the end of 390 days on his side had come! But, the Word of the Lord was announcing the end of days for Jerusalem, Judah, and the house of Israel in the Promised Land. Ezekiel 7:1 – 27 foretells the certain doom of the nation and people of Israel. This is a dramatic, poetic chapter. There are illustrations from nature: a budding rod; from the business world: buyers and sellers; of a watchman: blowing a trumpet; of fearfulness and shame: mourning doves; and of worthless possessions: silver and gold.

Read Ezekiel 7:1-27. Be sure to notice each time the Lord states "then you shall know that I am the Lord."

List the ways "the end" is described throughout this chapter:

Ezekiel 7:2

Ezekiel 7:5-7

Ezekiel 7:10

Ezekiel 7:12

Ezekiel 7:19

Ezekiel 7:25, 26

Ezekiel 7:27

What a message! Ezekiel couldn't even begin this sermon with an announcement of "I've got good news and bad news. Which do you want to hear first?" because all he had was bad news.

What do you think could have been a headline for this breaking news story?

In the passage below, highlight every occurrence of the words *land* and *you* in one color, and *anger, repay* and *judge* in another color.

Ezekiel 7:2-9 "Thus says the Lord GOD to the land of Israel: 'An end! The end has come upon the four corners of the land. ³Now the end *has come* upon you, and I will send My anger against you; I will judge you according to your ways, and I will repay you for all your abominations. ⁴My eye will not spare you, nor will I have pity' but I will repay your ways, and your abominations will be in your midst; then you shall know that I am the LORD!" ⁵"Thus says the Lord GOD: 'A disaster, a singular disaster; behold, it has come! ⁶An end has come, the end has come; it has dawned for you; behold, it has come! Doom has come to you, you who dwell in the land; The time has come, a day of trouble is near, and not of rejoicing in the mountains. Now upon you I will soon pour out My fury, and spend My anger upon you; I will judge you according to your ways, and I will repay you for all your abominations. 'My eye will not spare, nor will I have pity; I will repay you according to your ways, and your abominations will be in your midst. Then you shall know that I am the LORD who strikes."

On whom is the Lord going to pour out His wrath? Why?

What will be the results of the disastrous day described here? You can include positive and negative outcomes.

Here's what this passage would sound like if it were delivered today:

GOD's Word came to me, saying,

> You, son of man--GOD, the Master, has this Message for the land of Israel: "Endtime. The end of business as usual for everyone. It's all over. The end is upon you. I've launched my anger against you. I've issued my verdict on the way you live. I'll make you pay for your disgusting obscenities. I won't look the other way, I won't feel sorry for you. I'll make you pay for the way you've lived: Your disgusting obscenities will boomerang on you, and you'll realize that I am GOD.

I, GOD, the Master, say: Disaster after disaster! Look, it comes! Endtime -- the end comes. The end is ripe. Watch out, it's coming! This is your fate, you who live in this land. Time's up. It's zero hour. No dragging of feet now, no bargaining for more time. Soon now I'll pour my wrath on you, pay out my anger against you, Render my verdict on the way you've lived, make you pay for your disgusting obscenities. I won't look the other way, I won't feel sorry for you. I'll make you pay for the way you've lived. Your disgusting obscenities will boomerang on you. Then you'll realize that it is I, GOD, who has hit you.

Judgment Day! Fate has caught up with you. The scepter outsized and pretentious, pride bursting all bounds, violence strutting, brandishing the evil scepter. But there's nothing to them, and nothing will be left of them.

Time's up. Countdown: five, four, three, two . . . Buyer, don't crow; seller, don't worry: Judgment wrath has turned the world topsy-turvy. The bottom has dropped out of buying and selling. It will never be the same again. But don't fantasize an upturn in the market. The country is bankrupt because of its sins, and it's not going to get any better.

The trumpet signals the call to battle: 'Present arms!' But no one marches into battle. My wrath has them paralyzed! On the open roads you're killed, or else you go home and die of hunger and disease. Either get murdered out in the country or die of sickness or hunger in town. Survivors run for the hills. They moan like doves in the valleys, Each one moaning for his own sins. Every hand hangs limp, every knee turns to rubber.

They dress in rough burlap -- sorry scarecrows, shifty and shamefaced, with their heads shaved bald. They throw their money into the gutters. Their hard-earned cash stinks like garbage. They find that it won't buy a thing they either want or need on Judgment Day. They tripped on money and fell into sin. Proud and pretentious with their jewels, they deck out their vile and vulgar no-gods in finery. I'll make those god-obscenities a stench in their nostrils. I'll give away their religious junk-- strangers will pick it up for free, the godless spit on it and make jokes.

I'll turn my face so I won't have to look as my treasured place and people are violated, as violent strangers walk in and desecrate place and people -- a bloody massacre, as crime and violence fill the city. I'll bring in the dregs of humanity to move into their houses. I'll put a stop to the boasting and strutting of the high-and-mighty, and see to it that there'll be nothing holy left in their holy places.

Catastrophe descends. They look for peace, but there's no peace to be found -- disaster on the heels of disaster, one rumor after another. They clamor for the prophet to tell them what's up, but nobody knows anything. Priests don't have a clue; the elders don't know what to say.

The king holds his head in despair; the prince is devastated. The common people are paralyzed. Gripped by fear, they can't move. I'll deal with them where they are, judge them on their terms. They'll know that I am GOD."   Ezekiel 7, from *The Message*

It is very important to clearly observe who this passage applies to: it was strictly spoken to the nation of Israel, and you have already seen in 2 Kings that the Lord carried out His judgment against them when Nebuchadnezzer of Babylon besieged the city, burned it, killed many, and took the rest into captivity. None of the verses in this chapter should be spoken to someone today as a threat of impending doom.

In this terrible message of doom, the Lord announces that "His eye will not spare nor will He have pity." It is hard to comprehend the Lord in this way. But He was keeping His word.

Look at the following verses and note what you learn.

Deuteronomy 29:14-21

Jeremiah 13:14

Lamentations 2:21

2 Peter 2:4-6

Based on the verses in 2 Peter, how should we look at the previous acts of the Lord's judgments?

This is very hard to grasp and accept. That the Lord would bring about destruction on that which He has created. From the angels, to the wicked in Noah's time, to the perverted in Sodom and Gomorrah, to His very own chosen people Israel and their land. But His very nature forces this action. He is holy, holy, holy.

Throughout our study of the book of Ezekiel, there will be many opportunities to consider the judgment of the Lord. There will be many opportunities to look at the wrath of God from our perspective which comes after the death and resurrection of Jesus Christ. But today, we will end the lesson considering the awesome, sovereign justice of the Lord.

Not only is it right for God to display anger against sin, I find it impossible to understand how he could do otherwise.[4]   A. W. TOZER (1897–1963)

Reviewing the Revelations

Unit Two

The Ominous Warning

Ezekiel 4—7

What were the most meaningful Scriptures or truths from this unit's lessons?

How do these truths impact your daily life?

Is there anything that you have questions about?

Prayer Requests and Praises

Today's Date:

My personal request:

Confidential requests from my friends:

Do not be anxious about anything, but in everything, by prayer and petition, with thanksgiving, present your requests to God.
Philippians 4:6 NIV

Notes

UNIT THREE
Travesty in the Temple

LESSON ONE
Idols Adored
EZEKIEL 8

LESSON TWO
Wicked Slain
EZEKIEL 9

LESSON THREE
Glory Departs
EZEKIEL 10

LESSON FOUR
Hope for the Hopeless
EZEKIEL 11

LESSON ONE *Idols Adored* EZEKIEL 8

Pray that you will see the holiness of the Lord as you study today.

יהוה

In our time machine this week we will do more traveling with Ezekiel. His mode of transport was the Spirit of the Lord. We too must be dependent on the Holy Spirit to lead us and teach us. In this unit, we will study Chapters 8-11 of Ezekiel and see amazing things in the Word of God. We concluded our previous studies considering the sovereign justice of the Lord. We will continue to see His righteous wrath throughout the book of Ezekiel, but we will also see the Lord's plans for Israel, plans to prosper them, and plans to give them a future and a hope.

Please read Ezekiel 8:1-11:25. This is basically in a narrative, story form. You won't understand everything at first, but reading through these chapters will give you a good overall perspective. It's good news and bad news for the Israelites; persevere in your reading, the good news is in Chapter 11!

What is your initial reaction to what you have just read?

Today we will focus on Ezekiel 8, and then the following chapters during our next days of study. While Chapter 8 is full of supernatural images, it's easy to make basic observations from this chapter.

From Ezekiel 8:1, please note the following details:

Who is mentioned:

What happened:

When did this happen:

Where did this take place:

You can learn quite a few things from this one verse! Consider the location, the timing, and who was present. What conclusions and personal applications can you draw from these details?

Ezekiel was moved by the hand of the Lord and it was no gentle push. It was more like a tidal wave!

Please read Ezekiel 8:2-4 then summarize what happened when the hand of the Lord fell upon Ezekiel.

The words used in this passage seem to indicate that Ezekiel was actually physically removed from his house and carried to Jerusalem . . . by his hair! But if we look closely at a few words, we will see that Ezekiel never left Babylon.

Please locate the words below in Ezekiel 8:2-4, then look up their meanings:

Looked: Strong's #7200

Hebrew word:

Hebrew definition:

Visions: Strong's #4759

Hebrew word:

Hebrew definition:

Vision: Strong's #4758

Hebrew word:

Hebrew definition:

All of what we will study in Ezekiel 8-11 occurred during a vision of God. Please look up "vision" in a Bible dictionary and note what you learn.

Based on the word definitions and information above, how would you explain what Ezekiel experienced?

While Ezekiel's visions were more like virtual reality, and probably did not involve actual physical movement, they definitely involved spiritual reality. Do you think anyone could have convinced Ezekiel that he just imagined what he saw? I don't. When you have an encounter with the Living God, you know that He Is.

The stage is set now to join Ezekiel on his tour through the temple led by the Lord.

List each of the images from Ezekiel 8:3-16 that the Lord shows Ezekiel that defile the sanctuary of the Lord and demonstrate the wickedness of the people of Israel. Note the locations and directions which are mentioned. On the plan of the temple at the bottom of the page, mark each place to which Ezekiel is taken and illustrate what the Lord shows him in each place.

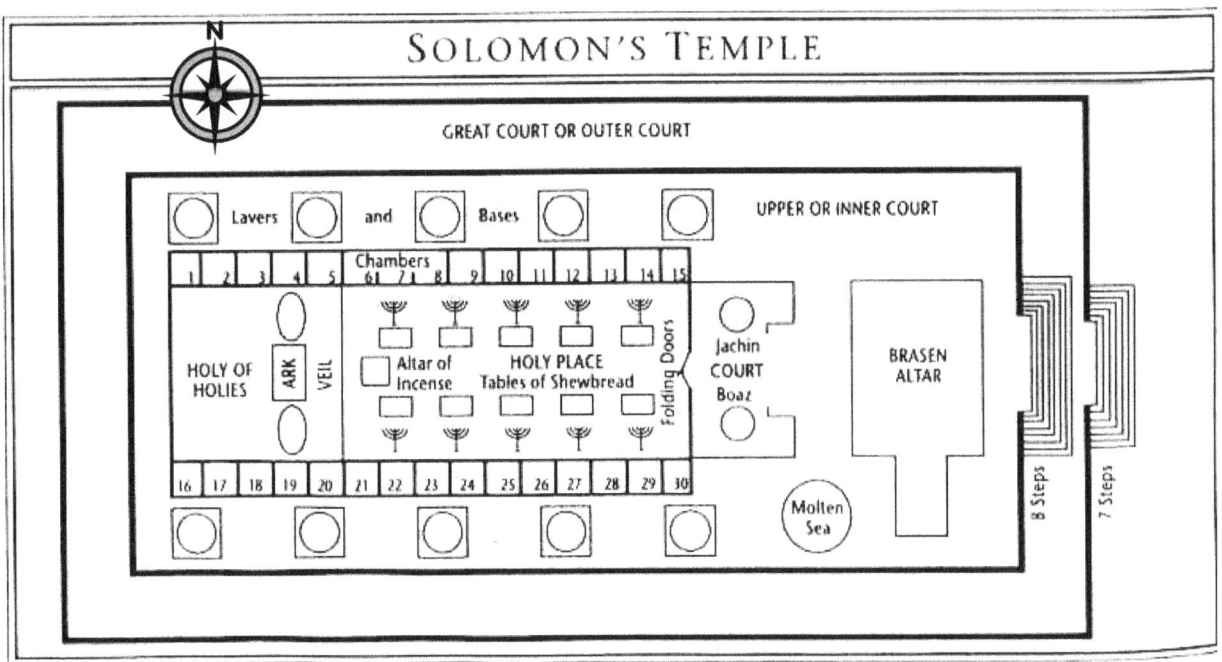

A little research will shed a lot of light on the figures and actions described above. Look up the meaning of the words below and how their meanings add to your understanding of the verses in which they are found.

Abominations, Ezekiel 8:6: Strong's #8441

Hebrew word:

Hebrew definition:

Creeping things, Ezekiel 8:7-11: Strong's #7431

Hebrew word:

Hebrew definition:

Beasts, Ezekiel 8:10: Strong's #929

Hebrew word:

Hebrew definition:

Look at Leviticus 11:24-31. Consider the instruction given in these verses, and then what you have just read in Ezekiel 8:7-11. What are your impressions of the actions of the Israelites?

Look in a Bible dictionary for an explanation of "Tammuz." Note what you find and how it adds to your understanding of Ezekiel 8:13-14.

Read Ezekiel 8:15-16 then note what instructions were given to the Israelites in Deuteronomy 4:15-19.

The following word describes the action taken by the 25 men in Ezekiel 8:16. What does it mean and what do you think about this action taking place inside the temple walls?

Worshipped: Strong's #7812

Hebrew word:

Hebrew definition:

Read through Ezekiel 8:6-18 once more. How many times does the Lord say "Do you see, " or "see," or "have you seen."

What do the elders of Israel say in Ezekiel 8:12?

Oh, the Lord sees. Nothing is hidden from Him. He showed Ezekiel the revolting acts of worship committed by the elders of Israel, the women of Israel, and the priests of Israel that He had been observing for years. The idolatrous worship increased in intensity from being done in secret to being done in public to being committed in the Lord's own temple.

How did the Lord react? Describe His declaration made in Ezekiel 8:17-18.

How do you react to what you've just seen described in this chapter?

It's easy to be appalled at the idolatrous worship committed by the Israelites long ago. Hindsight gives 20/20 vision. But the vision that the Lord gave Ezekiel was not hindsight. It was a vision of the practices in the present.

Do you have vision, sight, and awareness of practices today which provoke the Lord to anger? What actions might Christians be involved in today that are directly disobedient to the Word of God?

Please take a moment and allow the Holy Spirit to show you if you are committing any acts of idolatry against the Lord. Conviction is uncomfortable, but it's far better than discipline.

I grieve over the times that I have turned my back on the Lord. He's more wonderful than anything else I could ever turn to. He's so wonderful that He calls me to return to Him. Even though we will continue to see His judgment on Israel, the whole point of the Lord's messages to Ezekiel is to encourage His people to return to Him.

LESSON TWO   *Wicked Slain*   **EZEKIEL 9**

Please take time to pray before you study today. Studying the judgment of the Lord against the people of Israel will be challenging to our hearts and minds.

יהוה

We are about to look closely at Ezekiel 9. We definitely need a clear reminder of what the elders, women, and even priests of Israel were doing that brought about the extreme judgment that we will see carried out in this chapter.

Please read Ezekiel 8:1-9:2.

Based on the previous study, please summarize from Ezekiel 8 what Ezekiel was shown in and around the temple of the Lord.

The Lord abides by His own law that He has given the people. There was a legal reason for showing Ezekiel the wicked actions of the Israelites. What does John 7:51 say?

The law was given by the Lord through Moses and was very specific. Please note what you learn from Deuteronomy 19:15, 20-21.

In Ezekiel 9 we will see the wrath of God revealed from heaven against all ungodliness and unrighteousness. Please turn to Romans 1:21-23. This passage provides a commentary on unrighteous actions. Note those which parallel the heart and mind of the ancient Israelites.

Now please read Ezekiel 9 in its entirety. As you read, pay attention to the various groups of people that are mentioned, as well as the instructions or actions that correlate to them. Note everything that you can find that describes the following people, including the instructions or actions pertaining to them.

Six men

One man

Men who sigh

Old and young men, maidens and little children and women

Who were these six men plus one who came at the command of the Lord, who came ready to strike down those who committed great abominations in the city? The Hebrew word for "those who have charge" is pequddah. Its meanings include oversight, custody, and visitation. The word also signifies the arrangement of fighting men under an officer.

Commentaries give two possible explanations for the identity of these men. They may have been angels commissioned to carry out the punishment dictated by the Lord, or they may have been members of Nebuchadnezzar's army, his princes or officers, used by the Lord to judge the sins of the people of Israel.

If only one word could be used to define the sins which the Lord showed Ezekiel in the temple, it would be the word idolatry. The Lord's reaction and punishment on His people for their idolatry is similar in this situation to His reaction to the worship of the golden calf made by Aaron when Moses was on Mount Sinai.

Read Exodus 32:25-28, 33-35 and note the similarities you see to Ezekiel 9.

Are you ready for some relief from the killing? Ezekiel 9:4 shows that the Lord knew "whoever was on the Lord's side," and He prepared special protection for them.

Look up the meaning for the following word:

Mark: Strong's #8420

Hebrew word:

Hebrew definition:

Are there other references of the Lord's special markings coming to mind? Let's take a moment to consider them. Look at the following verses and note what type of mark is made and its purpose.

Genesis 4:13-15

Exodus 12:12-13

Ephesians 1:13

Revelation 7:3

Here's an exciting bit of trivia from the Jamieson Fausset Brown commentary on Ezekiel 9:4:

> **A mark**--literally, the Hebrew letter Tau, the last in the alphabet, used as a mark; originally written in the form of a cross! In Ezekiel 9:4, we see that those who sigh and cry over all the abominations done in Jerusalem are the ones who receive the mark of protection and deliverance.[2]

Psalm 119:136 describes the grief of those sighing well. Why did they cry?

Isaiah 57:15 further describes the heart and soul of the one with whom the Lord will dwell. What is the Lord looking for?

When we recognize our own sin and grieve over it, the Lord is ready to forgive and heal us. According to the following verses, what does Jesus Christ do?

Matthew 5:3-4

Luke 4:18

James 4:6

*The Lord said to Ezekiel: "My eye will neither spare, not will I have pity, but I will recompense their deeds on their own head." We have just looked at the heart of those who received the mark of deliverance. It was their lifestyle **before** the time of judgment that spared those who were marked. They grieved over the sins of their brethren, and they had not participated in them.*

What can you learn from this example?

What should you do in the face of the constant temptations of the world? What is promised in 2 Peter 2:9?

What are some of the ways that you have seen the Lord deliver you out of temptations? How do you know when He is providing deliverance? How do you respond?

We can't finish our study of Ezekiel 9 until we've looked at Ezekiel's first comment since the time that he was told to bake his bread over human waste. He had quite a few incredible instructions and experiences in chapters 1 through 8, yet he has only spoken once.

What does he do and say now in response to the killing of so many from the house of Israel and Judah?

Ezekiel was following the example of God's chosen and humble servants who had lived before him. Look at the following verses and note the circumstances and actions taken by Moses, Abraham, and David.

Genesis 18:22-27

Numbers 16:20-22

1 Chronicles 21:16-17

Ezekiel was interceding for his people, his nation, his heritage and his future. How often are you burdened in such a way? How often do you pray for the Lord to deliver your family and friends? Your community? Your country?

> If my people, who are called by my name, will humble themselves and pray and seek my face and turn from their wicked ways, then will I hear from heaven and will forgive their sin and will heal their land.   2 Chronicles 7:14-15

We have seen in Ezekiel 8 and 9 that iniquity, bloodshed, and committing abominations were the normal lifestyles of the Israelites. Take a look at your local newspaper today and see if you think people have changed any over the years. I expect that you will agree that the culture and societal norms today are just as bad as they were back in time.

Please take this opportunity to intercede for those you know and even those you don't know. Pray that they will know and fear the Lord.

May the Lord use this lesson in our lives to keep us sensitive to His holiness and the worship that is due Him, and the seriousness of sin in our own lives and in the lives of those around us. When we report to the Lord on that future day, may we say as the one clothed in linen said: "I have done as You commanded me."

LESSON THREE   *Glory Departs*   EZEKIEL 10

Please pray that the Holy Spirit will lead you in your study today to know the Lord more closely through relationship, not through religion.

יהוה

The first exercise in our first lesson was to read Ezekiel 8:1-11:25 so that you would have an initial overview of the events that Ezekiel witnessed. Now that we have studied Ezekiel 8 and 9, you have a deeper understanding of them. The events you witnessed in these two chapters result in a terrible consequence described in Ezekiel 10.

Please read Ezekiel 8:1-10:22.

Take a moment and consider the privilege that we have to read the visible Word of God which reveals the invisible glory of God to us. Our study today will focus on our infinite, invisible, incomprehensible Lord.

Please list each description of the Lord from your reading so that you can trace His presence and movement as described in these three chapters. It will be helpful to make notes in two columns below. You have already noticed in your reading that there is a detailed description of the cherubim in Ezekiel 10. You don't have to list their detailed appearance at this time, but you will need to observe the location of the glory of the Lord in relation to them. Begin in Ezekiel 8:1 and continue through 10:22.

Appearance   **Location**

Location, location, location! It's often the most important thing in business, home, and school. The repetition of the locations of the abominations and the locations of the glory of the Lord should show us the importance of what was happening at the temple. In previous chapters of Ezekiel we saw idolatrous worship committed on high places and under the trees. We saw that the city of Jerusalem would be under siege because of the iniquity of the people. We saw that the whole land would be devastated because of rebelliousness. In Ezekiel 8, 9, and 10, the location of judgment is the very dwelling place of the Lord, His holy temple.

Here is the depiction of the house of the Lord again. From your notes, illustrate the movement of the glory of the Lord based on what you recorded in the previous exercise.

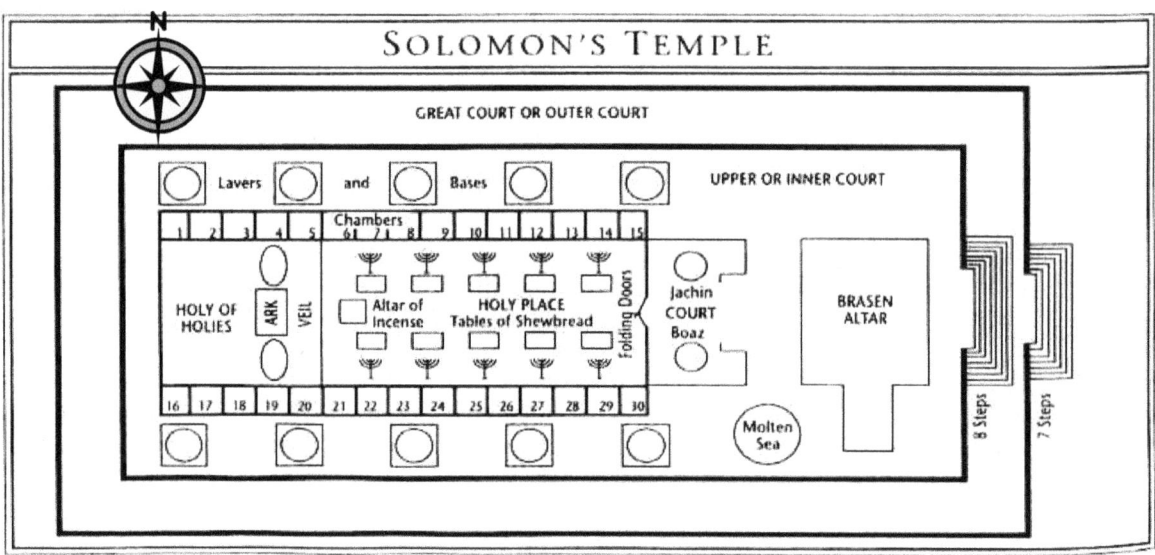

That which we are studying in Ezekiel, the depravity of the people, the destruction of Jerusalem and the departure of the presence of the Lord are the extreme judgments of the Lord. Even more extreme than the destruction of the world by flood or the devastation of Sodom and Gomorrah.

Let's look back at the early days of the temple. King David had desired to build a house for the Lord, but was told that his son Solomon would do so instead. The Lord gave David the plans for the temple, and David prepared them and passed them on to Solomon. After seven years of building, the temple was completed and dedicated.

Please read the following passages and note the purpose of the temple as well as what happened at the time of its dedication.

2 Chronicles 2:3-5

2 Chronicles 5:11-6:2

2 Chronicles 6:40-7:3

*Surely the presence of the Lord was in **that** place!*

The Lord responded to the prayer and dedication made by Solomon by arriving on the scene. And then He spoke. What promises, expectations, and consequences did the Lord communicate in 2 Chronicles 7:15-22?

Do you see that the Lord God spoke His word clearly to His people? Previously we looked at a few verses in Romans that paralleled the hearts and minds of the house of Israel. Please read the passage in its entirety now: Romans 1:18-32. Note the way that the Lord carries out His judgment on unrighteousness. What do you see in this passage in Romans regarding the acts of the people and the reaction of the Lord that is similar to what we have seen in Ezekiel?

"Since the creation of the world, His invisible attributes are clearly seen...." Yet foolish men have "changed the glory of the incomprehensible God into an image made like corruptible man." The Lord has made Himself known in so many ways; no one needs to craft images out of wood and stone. In Jesus Christ all the fullness of the Godhead dwells in human form.

How did the disciple John describe his encounter with the Lord? Record what you learn from 1 John 1:1-2.

What does Colossians 1:15-18 say about Jesus?

There was a day in the distant past when the invisible God showed Himself as a thick cloud that filled the temple. Then there was the night in the past when the invisible God showed Himself as a baby whose birth filled the skies with joy. I hope you have experienced a time in your life when the invisible God showed Himself to you as your Savior and His Spirit filled your soul.

Please note who you are and the desire of the Lord according to the following verses:

1 Corinthians 3:16-17

1 Corinthians 6:18-20

2 Corinthians 6:14-7:1

I hope you are rejoicing over the amazing choice of the Lord for His dwelling place today. There is a very important difference in His plan for residency in believers as compared to His plan to dwell in the temple.

The Lord's home in the previous temple was based on conditional promises which we looked at in 2 Chronicles. What promises do you see in the next verses?

John 14:20-23

Matthew 28:20

Hebrews 13:5-6

There is one more temple that we should visit today. Please read John 2:13-17. Note the "abominations" being carried out and the reaction of Christ to them.

What did the disciples remember from Scripture?

Look up the meaning for the following word:

Zeal: Strong's #2205

Greek word:

Greek definition:

Why does the Lord express Himself with such great passion? You'll find the answer as you look at the following verses.

Deuteronomy 32:16, 21

Isaiah 42:8

Jeremiah 31:3

We've done a lot of traveling through time today. From Ezekiel's time to Solomon's time to the time of Christ and to our own time as well. Please return to Ezekiel 10 and read this chapter once again. It seems to me that the Lord moved very slowly out of the temple.

Based on all that we have looked at today, what have you learned about the temple and the glory of the Lord?

> The presence of God in the sanctuary was a great privilege for the people of Israel, but it was also a great responsibility. The glory of God cannot dwell with the sins of God's people, so it was necessary for the glory to leave and the sanctuary and the people to be judged.[3]
>
> WARREN WIERSBE

Look at the following Psalms and choose the one which best expresses your heart regarding the house of the Lord. Write out the verse and spend time dedicating yourself as the Lord's temple, His dwelling place today.

Psalm 5:7

Psalm 23:6

Psalm 27:4

Psalm 122:1

LESSON FOUR — *Hope for the Hopeless* — EZEKIEL 11

Prepare your heart for your study today, that you may know the LORD.

יהוה

Are you anticipating your first assignment today? Yes, I will be asking you to read Ezekiel 11. But only that one chapter, for a change! If this chapter were a broadcast of the evening news, I'd describe the schedule like this:

> *Ezekiel 11:1-4: Bad news*
>
> *Ezekiel 11:5-12: More bad news*
>
> *Ezekiel 11:13: The reporter's reaction*
>
> *Ezekiel 11:14-18: The good news*
>
> *Ezekiel 11:19, 20: The best news of the day*
>
> *Ezekiel 11:21-23: Emergency broadcast*
>
> *Ezekiel 11:24-25: The reporter's review*

It's your turn. Please read Ezekiel 11, and then outline this chapter in your own creative format. It may be more like a Greek tragedy than a newscast. Or perhaps a dramatic novel. Maybe a poem or a ballad. There is something it is not: a lighthearted comedy or vaudeville act.

Who are the first participants that we see in this chapter of Ezekiel's life? (Ezekiel 11:1-4) What does the Lord say about them, and what do they say about their circumstances?

"The city is the caldron, and we are the meat." (Ezekiel 11:3) I haven't heard anyone use that analogy recently! That was the perspective of the leaders of the city. The Lord was a master communicator through His prophet Ezekiel. He turned the analogy around to give the leaders the true perspective of their circumstances.

Look at a few commentaries and note the explanation of the phrase used in Ezekiel 11:3, 7 and 11. What were the leaders trying to communicate to the people in Jerusalem?

"Prophesy against them, prophesy, O son of man!" (Ezekiel 11:4) Do you sense passion in this instruction? What happens immediately following this statement? What is the message that Ezekiel is to speak to the princes of Jerusalem? Consider Ezekiel 11:5-12 and record your findings.

How would you respond if the Lord gave you an assignment to speak words of truth such as these? Have you ever been in a situation where you had to confront someone with their sinful actions or attitudes? What can you learn from the example given here?

We see Ezekiel's third response to the Lord in verse 13. The Lord gives him much to say, but he doesn't say much to the Lord. His comments are rare but extraordinary.

How did Ezekiel respond to the Lord's prophecy and the death of Pelatiah?

Look up the meaning for the following words:

Pelatiah: Strong's #6410 see also root word: Strong's #6403

Hebrew word:

Hebrew definition:

Do you see the connection between the death of Pelatiah and the question asked by Ezekiel? He had been commissioned to confront his people, the Israelites, with their sin. But he was deeply grieved that the Lord might completely destroy the nation. Look back at your answer to the personal question above regarding speaking truth and confronting others.

Do you confront with the words of the Holy Spirit, with a true burden for them, with a desire to see change, or do you want to see the judgment of the Lord destroy them?

There is a book called <u>Caring Enough to Confront</u>, by David Augsberger. I recommend it to you for a thorough instruction in how to have a caring conversation with someone regarding difficult times. He says:

> I grow most rapidly when supported with the arm of loving respect, then confronted with the arm of clear honesty. Confronting and caring stimulate growth. This is how God relates to us. When we speak of God's relationship with man we have historically used other words. Judgment and grace lead to salvation.
>
> God's judgment - radical honesty about truth - confronts us with the demands of disciplined maturity. God's grace - undeserved love - reaches out to accept and affirm us at the point we know ourselves to be unacceptable.
>
> Judgment cuts, even kills. If God dwelt with us only in judgment, who could stand? If God reached out to us only in love, it would be a cheap grace without integrity. Mere divine permissiveness. "Anything goes" as far as heaven is concerned. Not so!
>
> Judgment blended with grace. Confrontation matched with caring. Truth spoken in love. Honesty, truth, trust, and love. These all interlock and intertwine in the biblical statements on relationships.[4]

The principles Augsberger outlines in the first chapter of his book are demonstrated in Ezekiel 11. We are about to look at the love and grace offered by the Lord after His truthful declaration of judgment. Most of the book of Ezekiel declares the "radical honesty about truth" and "the demands of disciplined maturity." Most of the book of Ezekiel clearly states the judgment of the Lord, but love and grace are declared as well, albeit sparingly. It does stand out as the best news of the day!

In Ezekiel 11:16-20, because of His love and grace, the Lord gives several promises of new and wonderful things for the house of Israel. List them below. Break them down into the "step-by-step" explanation that the Lord gives.

The first promise given by the Lord is amazing in light of the context of Chapter 10 and Chapter 11, verse 23. Look ahead to Ezekiel 11:22-23 and note the movement of the glory of the Lord. What impact do you think the Lord's promise in Ezekiel 11:16 would have on Ezekiel and the exiles in Babylon?

Mark on your list on the previous page, perhaps with different colored highlighters, the actions that the Lord will take for the people, and the actions the people will take in response to the Lord.

What do you think about the response of the Israelites? Isn't this what the Lord has been asking them to do for their entire history as a nation? Why will they do it "then?" The answer to that question is life-changing, both for the Israelites and for us. The Lord announced through Ezekiel His plan to make a new covenant with His people. The Jews living at the time of Christ had the first opportunity to receive new hearts and spirits. Some did. Others didn't. Then the Lord offered this new covenant to the Gentiles. Today, we can be recipients of a miraculous heart transplant!

The Lord had already told the Israelites, long ago that they needed surgery on their heart. What did He say in Deuteronomy 10:16 and 30:6?

Many years later the Lord said the same thing through Ezekiel's contemporary. What did He say in Jeremiah 4:4?

Now turn to Colossians 2:11-14 to see the cutting away of the old heart and the transplant of the new. According to these scriptures, how is the heart circumcised? What is involved? What is the result?

Look at these Scriptures for further details of this change of heart and note what you learn:

John 3:6

2 Corinthians 5:17

Ephesians 4:22-24

This is no less than death to self. A funeral for the sin nature. The destruction of a sinner and the resurrection of a saint. At the time of salvation, the surgery is performed. At the cross, the old self is crucified with Christ.

Go ahead – check me on this – turn to Romans 6:5-11. Make a few notes of the details of the death of the old man from this passage.

Now, please turn to Galatians 2:20 and write out, word for word, this truth. Notice that it is in first person and applies to everyone who believes in Jesus Christ as her Savior.

If you have never attended the funeral of your old self, please, do so now. If you have been keeping that old, stone cold heart around your neck as a souvenir, let it go! Bury it! It's always been dead. It would never start working again! You had to have a brand new heart, just like the Israelites! And praise the Lord, He gave you one! Filled with His Holy Spirit. You are alive in Christ! Hallelujah!

We started today's study with a news broadcast. It's time now to write a notice for the obituaries of the newspaper. There isn't much good to say about the old self, but declare it dead. You knew it well. Be honest with your description of who you used to be. This may turn out to be the first day of the rest of your life!

The dearest idol I have known, Whate'er that idol be,
Help me to tear it from thy throne, And worship only thee.[5]

WILLIAM COWPER (1731–1800)

Reviewing the Revelations

Unit Three

Travesty in the Temple

Ezekiel 8-11

What were the most meaningful Scriptures or truths from this unit's lessons?

How do these truths impact your daily life?

Is there anything that you have questions about?

Prayer Requests and Praises

Today's Date:

My personal request:

Confidential requests from my friends:

Be joyful always; pray continually; give thanks in all circumstances,

For this is God's will for you in Christ Jesus.

1 Thessalonians 5:16-18 NIV

Notes

UNIT FOUR

The Truth Is Told

LESSON ONE
Sign Language
EZEKIEL 12:1-21

LESSON TWO
Deceptive Declarations
EZEKIEL 12:21-28

LESSON THREE
False Forecasters
EZEKIEL 13

LESSON FOUR
Hypocrites and Heroes
EZEKIEL 14:1-11

LESSON ONE — *Sign Language* — EZEKIEL 12:1-21

Please pray that the Holy Spirit will lead you in understanding the Word of the Lord today.

𐤉𐤄𐤅𐤄

We are about to look at two very interesting visual sermons that the Lord gave Ezekiel to preach to his fellow exiles. Chapter 12 opens with the reminder that the people are blind and deaf to the truth from the Lord and it ends with a strong declaration from the Lord that "the word which He speaks will be done" even if the Israelites don't believe it. There are principles in this chapter which will be applicable to our own lives today and we will discover them while we look at the actions of the radical prophet Ezekiel.

Please read Ezekiel 12:1-2 and note the important details that are given to you in these verses.

Please turn back to page 20, and look at the description of the house of Israel listed there. Also review your answers to the questions about your impressions of Ezekiel's commission, and your thoughts on the way the Lord described the house of Israel. Record a brief summary of your thoughts here.

Now that Ezekiel has been shown the detailed visions of the people's idolatrous worship, and he has heard their false prophecy, do you think that he is convinced of this description of his fellow Israelites? How do you think he feels about his commission to preach to the rebellious house of Israel now?

If you were in Ezekiel's sandals, how would you react to receiving this commission to preach to a hard-hearted people who wouldn't see or hear the truth?

Let's see how the Lord instructs Ezekiel to communicate to the blind and deaf. He uses sign language! Read Ezekiel 12:3-6 and list each instruction from the Lord.

Read Ezekiel 12:7 and list Ezekiel's response to his instructions from the Lord. Be thorough and list everything he did.

Read Ezekiel 12:8-14 and make notes of the important details or explanations given in these verses.

Circle, highlight, or mark the word "captivity" each time it is mentioned in Ezekiel 12:1-14.

What is the main message that the Lord is communicating to the Israelites in Babylon through this illustration?

"Thus says the Lord God: 'None of My words will be postponed any more, but the word which I speak will be done,; says the Lord God" (Ezekiel 12:28) The rebellious house of Israel didn't believe the warnings, the messages or the judgments that were spoken through the many prophets sent by the Lord. But as we have already seen, the Lord was keeping His word according to His own timing. The last date that we were given by Ezekiel in his "journal" was the sixth year, in the sixth month, on the fifth day of the month. (Ezekiel 8:1) This was approximately 592 B.C. The visual sermon we have just looked at is believed to have been received in the same year, because no other dates are given. Then six years later, in 586 B.C., the prophecy regarding the exile and captivity of the "prince" came to pass.

Turn to 2 Kings 25:1-7 and Jeremiah 39:1-7 to see the historical account which fulfilled the prophecy given through Ezekiel years before it happened. Note the parallels between Ezekiel's action sermon and the actual event.

The next visual illustration preached by Ezekiel was probably delivered shortly after the portrayal of the king going into captivity. You already know "the rest of the story," but keep in mind that the Babylonian exiles did not. They were living under false hopes due to false prophets. This illustration will communicate the certainty of the coming judgment of the Lord.

Read Ezekiel 12:17-20, summarize the action sermon Ezekiel is to give, and explain the message that the Lord wanted to communicate to the exiles through this sermon.

Dr. J. Vernon McGee (1904-1988) was a preacher who taught with down-to-earth comments about the Word of God. He said "Ezekiel was a very brilliant man, but I think he also had a real sense of humor. I would love to have seen his face when he went through some of these mechanics! I think he might have been somewhat of a ham actor and been greatly amused as he did these things." [1]

Regarding the visual message we have just looked at, Dr. McGee says: "This is quite a stunt Ezekiel is going to pull. He is to bring his table out into the street and sit there, trembling as he eats. Then the people will come and say, 'What's the matter with you? Have you got a chill, or is it something you ate?' Ezekiel will give them God's message: 'I want you to know what's happening over yonder in Jerusalem. There's a famine over there. There's fear over there. God is destroying the city.' What an awesome message he has to bring." [2]

In a previous exercise, you looked at 2 Kings 25 to see the fulfillment of the prophecy of King Zedekiah being taken into captivity. If you look closely at this passage, you will also see the fulfillment of the sermon of the shaking and quaking eater.

Read the passage below and mark the dates given. Calculate the period of time in which the city was under siege.

2 Kings 25:1-3 "Now it came to pass in the ninth year of his reign, in the tenth month, on the tenth day of the month, that Nebuchadnezzar king of Babylon and all his army came against Jerusalem and encamped against it; and they built a siege wall against it all around. So the city was besieged until the eleventh year of King Zedekiah. By the ninth day of the fourth month the famine had become so severe in the city that there was no food for the people of the land."

Using your imagination, describe what you think it would have been like to live in the city of Jerusalem during the time of the siege.

The Lord knew exactly what it would be like for His chosen people living in His Holy city during the time of the siege of Nebuchadnezzar. He warned them repeatedly of what was to come through prophets like Joel, Isaiah and Jeremiah. He offered them a way of escape but they would not listen to Him.

I see two ways to personally apply this message of the Word of God to our own lives. First, consider what the Lord has warned you or instructed you about that you are ignoring or rejecting. He knows the path that you are on and what will come as a result. He offers deliverance to you, but you must obey His Word.

Is there anything that the Lord has communicated to you through His word that you have turned blind eyes and deaf ears toward?

If so, turn to Isaiah 55:6-7 for the Lord's message to you.

Second, notice that Ezekiel was instructed to deliver the Lord's message in very strange ways. Unusual. Eccentric. Radical.

Turn to Isaiah 55:8-9 and record the Lord's explanation of why He does what He does.

Is there anything that the Lord has called you to do that just doesn't seem to make sense? Is it unusual? Eccentric? Radical? If the instruction is not contradicted by any command given in the written Word of God, then you just may be being entrusted with a special assignment which will result in the glory of the Lord!

Please conclude today's lesson by praying and praising God by reading the verse below.

> Oh, the depth of the riches both of the wisdom and knowledge of God!
> How unsearchable are His judgments and His ways past finding out!
>
> For who has known the mind of the Lord? Or who has become His counselor?
>
> Or who has first given to Him and it shall be repaid to him?
>
> For of Him and through Him and to Him are all things, to whom be glory forever. Amen.   Romans 11:33-36

LESSON TWO   *Deceptive Declarations*   EZEKIEL 12:21-28

The Word of God has been given to you. Pray that you will believe it.

יהוה

The Lord allowed me to set aside this lesson of study specifically for Ezekiel 12:21-28. While this passage was clearly a direct message to the exiles in Babylon, even today it has a clear and direct message to us. I look forward to what we will learn of the Lord and His Word today and I hope you do too!

Read Ezekiel 12:21-28 below.

Please circle, highlight, or mark each occurrence of "the word of the Lord," "words," "proverb," "says," and "speak" as well as corresponding pronouns. List below what you learn about the Word of the Lord from the words that you have marked.

Ezekiel 12:21-28 21: And the word of the LORD came unto me, saying, 22 Son of man, what is that proverb that ye have in the land of Israel, saying, The days are prolonged, and every vision faileth? 23 Tell them therefore, Thus saith the Lord GOD; I will make this proverb to cease, and they shall no more use it as a proverb in Israel; but say unto them, The days are at hand, and the effect of every vision. 24 For there shall be no more any vain vision nor flattering divination within the house of Israel. 25 For I am the LORD: I will speak, and the word that I shall speak shall come to pass; it shall be no more prolonged: for in your days, O rebellious house, will I say the word, and will perform it, saith the Lord GOD. 26 Again the word of the LORD came to me, saying, 27 Son of man, behold, they of the house of Israel say, The vision that he seeth is for many days to come, and he prophesieth of the times that are far off. 28 Therefore say unto them, Thus saith the Lord GOD; There shall none of my words be prolonged any more, but the word which I have spoken shall be done, saith the Lord GOD.

Look up the meaning for the following word:

Proverb: Strong's #4912

Hebrew word:

Hebrew definition:

What specifically are the two "proverbs" that the Israelites are repeating to each other *as* truth?

What "proverbs" does the Lord speak which **are** the truth?

There are several other times that the word *mashal* is used in Ezekiel's book. Please look at the following verses and note what you observe about the use of proverbs. We will look further into the meanings of specific proverbs when we come to them later in our studies.

Ezekiel 14:8

Ezekiel 16:44

Ezekiel 17:2

Ezekiel 18:2-3

Ezekiel 20:49

Ezekiel 24:3

How would you summarize the use of proverbs in the life of the Israelites and in the life of Ezekiel?

How would you describe the use of proverbs, clichés, mottos and slogans in our life today?

On a website for English as a Second Language students, there is simple but excellent definition given for a proverb: it is a well-known short saying.[3] *The website lists 230 proverbs that most native English speakers know. These are a few random selections.*

A fool and his money are soon parted.

Actions speak louder than words.

To err is human.

A man is known by his friends.

Something is better than nothing.

Every picture tells a story.

Time is money.

Never too old to learn.

Today's proverbs, as well as ancient proverbs, at their best are based on truth, but sometimes they are based on truth viewed from a human perspective rather than from the Lord's perspective. And that's the wrong way to look at it!

Turn to Proverbs 1:1-7 and write the biblical definition which is given for a proverb. What is the crucial factor in order to have knowledge to understand proverbs?

We must know Who the Lord is and believe that He is Who He says He is. This is the basic attitude of one who fears the Lord.

Please turn back to Ezekiel 12:25 and record what you learn about the Lord from this verse.

Let's look at some other verses where the Lord declares Who He is and what He does. He spoke passionately through the prophet Isaiah, but the Israelites did not listen. Note what you learn from the following verses.

Isaiah 44:6-8

Isaiah 45:19

Isaiah 46:10-11

Isaiah 55:10-11

The Lord said to the Israelites: "You shall go out with joy, and be led out with peace; the mountains and the hills shall break forth into singing before you and all the trees of the field shall clap their hands!" (Isaiah 55:12) What joy comes from living according to the Word of God! Jesus gave the disciples the same motivation.

Please turn to John 15:9-11 and record what Jesus said about His words to His disciples.

Are you feeding on the nourishing Word of God, or are you snacking on empty proverbs? I need God's Word everyday. But there are some days when I let the details of life get in the way of spending time with the Lord through His Word, and I can always tell a difference in my life. My perspective starts to get influenced by my self, Satan, and the world. But, oh, the delight and refreshment and peace that comes from being with the Lord through His Word! I have learned to hear Him. I prayed for the Lord to open my eyes that I might behold wonderful things in His Word! He has answered that prayer!

What is your attitude toward the Word of God? Where are you in your pursuit of nourishment, fellowship, and true perspectives through the Word of God?

Because you are studying the unusual book of Ezekiel, I know that you are at least curious about God's Word! I hope that as we continue our study, your understanding of God's story and your knowledge of God's truth will grow deeper and deeper. Let's rejoice with what Peter wrote to the church:

> And so we have the prophetic word confirmed, which you do well to heed as a light that shines in a dark place, until the day dawns and the morning star rises in your hearts; knowing this first, that no prophecy of Scripture is of any private interpretation, for prophecy never came by the will of man, but holy men of God spoke as they were moved by the Holy Spirit. 2 Peter 1:19-21

Please return to Ezekiel 12:21-28 and once again read this passage. How would you summarize the message of the Lord to the Israelites?

Let's turn to the book that has the end of the story and the last words of the Lord. This is one more warning for all of us. Read Revelation 22:18-19. Note what the warning is and note any parallel you see to the Lord's message in Ezekiel 12:21-28.

His words are faithful and true. Blessed is he who keeps His words and looks forward to their fulfillment.

LESSON THREE   *False Forecasters*   **EZEKIEL 13**

Please take time to pray today to prepare your heart. Our own hearts can deceive us and we need to hear what the Lord says.

יהוה

Welcome to another message from the Lord to the rebellious house of Israel. Chapter 13 is an interesting one as it focuses on those who called themselves prophets and claimed to speak in the name of the Lord. In this chapter, you will see the Lord expose their selfish, sinful, and supernatural schemes. The Lord had just announced through Ezekiel that there would be no more of this foolish talk.(Ezekiel 12:24)

There is clear repetition of words and concepts throughout this chapter which emphasize the wicked actions of the so-called prophets and which also emphasize the Lord's response to their foolishness. Our first exercise will be to read Ezekiel 13 and mark repeated words, their corresponding pronouns, and repeated phrases. The passage is quoted on the next page for you. I recommend using four different colors and I also recommend marking all the repetitions of one word or concept first, then moving on to a different color.

First color: Mark every occurrence of "the word of the Lord" as well as occurrences of "say," "saying," "says," "spoken" and "thus says the Lord" in one color.

Second color: Mark every occurrence of "prophesy", "prophet", their corresponding pronouns (them, they their) as well as "Israel" and "women" and their and their corresponding pronouns. The prophets were of the house of Israel, and the women were self-styled prophetesses, not servants of the Lord.

Third color: Mark every occurrence of words or phrases that describe the false prophesy being spoken by the so-called prophets, "nothing", "futility", "false divination", "nonsense", "lies", etc.

Fourth color: Mark every occurrence of the phrase that the Lord gives as His ultimate purpose for carrying out judgment against the false prophets and house of Israel.

Ezekiel 13

¹And the word of the LORD came to me, saying, ² "Son of man, prophesy against the prophets of Israel who prophesy, and say to those who prophesy out of their own heart, 'Hear the word of the LORD!' "

³Thus says the Lord GOD: "Woe to the foolish prophets, who follow their own spirit and have seen nothing! ⁴O Israel, your prophets are like foxes in the deserts. ⁵You have not gone up into the gaps to build a wall for the house of Israel to stand in battle on the day of the LORD. ⁶They have envisioned futility and false divination, saying, 'Thus says the LORD!' But the LORD has not sent them; yet they hope that the word may be confirmed. ⁷Have you not seen a futile vision, and have you not spoken false divination? You say, 'The LORD says,' but I have not spoken."

⁸Therefore thus says the Lord GOD: "Because you have spoken nonsense and envisioned lies, therefore I am indeed against you," says the Lord GOD. ⁹ "My hand will be against the prophets who envision futility and who divine lies; they shall not be in the assembly of My people, nor be written in the record of the house of Israel, nor shall they enter into the land of Israel. Then you shall know that I am the Lord GOD.

¹⁰ "Because, indeed, because they have seduced My people, saying, 'Peace!' when there is no peace- and one builds a wall, and they plaster it with untempered mortar- ¹¹say to those who plaster it with untempered mortar, that it will fall. There will be flooding rain, and you, O great hailstones, shall fall; and a stormy wind shall tear it down. ¹²Surely, when the wall has fallen, will it not be said to you, 'Where is the mortar with which you plastered it?'"

¹³Therefore thus says the Lord GOD: "I will cause a stormy wind to break forth in My fury; and there shall be a flooding rain in My anger, and great hailstones in fury to consume

it. ¹⁴So I will break down the wall you have plastered with untempered mortar, and bring it down to the ground, so that its foundation will be uncovered; it will fall, and you shall be consumed in the midst of it. Then you shall know that I am the LORD.

¹⁵ "Thus will I accomplish My wrath on the wall and on those who have plastered it with untempered mortar; and I will say to you, 'The wall is no more, nor those who plastered it, ¹⁶that is, the prophets of Israel who prophesy concerning Jerusalem, and who see visions of peace for her when there is no peace,'" says the Lord GOD.

¹⁷ "Likewise, son of man, set your face against the daughters of your people, who prophesy out of their own heart; prophesy against them, ¹⁸and say, 'Thus says the Lord GOD: "Woe to the women who sew magic charms on their sleeves and make veils for the heads of people of every height to hunt souls! Will you hunt the souls of My people, and keep yourselves alive? ¹⁹And will you profane Me among My people for handfuls of barley and for pieces of bread, killing people who should not die, and keeping people alive who should not live, by your lying to My people who listen to lies?"

²⁰ 'Therefore thus says the Lord GOD: "Behold, I am against your magic charms by which you hunt souls there like birds. I will tear them from your arms, and let the souls go, the souls you hunt like birds. ²¹I will also tear off your veils and deliver My people out of your hand, and they shall no longer be as prey in your hand. Then you shall know that I am the LORD.

²² "Because with lies you have made the heart of the righteous sad, whom I have not made sad; and you have strengthened the hands of the wicked, so that he does not turn from his wicked way to save his life. ²³Therefore you shall no longer envision futility nor practice divination; for I will deliver My people out of your hand, and you shall know that I am the LORD."

Please make a list based on your markings of the description of the foolish prophets and what they said.

Can you imagine being one of these false prophets? Their description is despicable, but they were boldly speaking as if on behalf of the Lord. No wonder He said "enough!"

Let's look at the meaning of some of the words used to describe these deceivers and their words:

Foolish: Strong's #5036

Hebrew word:

Hebrew definition:

Futility: Strong's #7723 (Ezekiel 13:6)

Hebrew word:

Hebrew definition:

Divination: Strong's #7081

Hebrew word:

Hebrew definition:

The Lord compared the false prophets to foxes in the desert, and He also said that they "plastered with untempered mortar." Look in a commentary to find the explanation of these two analogies. What do they mean?

Matthew 23 is a complete chapter in the New Testament that parallels the heart of the Lord seen in Ezekiel 13. It is another condemnation of those who try to make themselves appear good but are inwardly wicked.

Please read Matthew 23:27-28. Who is described here, and what is their similarity to the false prophets being denounced in Ezekiel's day?

The Lord never failed to give His people His word which was for their good. Before Jesus delivered the "woes" to the scribes and Pharisees, He delivered solid words of truth and wisdom to them and to those following Him. His teaching in Matthew 7:24-29 is appropriate in light of the pronouncement made against the false prophets of Ezekiel's day. How does His teaching relate to what we are studying?

What do you think you need to be aware of in today's culture that could be equivalent to the false prophecies of Ezekiel's day?

After announcing His coming judgment on the false prophets, the Lord turned His attention and proclamations toward the women, the prophetesses, and the sorceresses who were basically practicing witchcraft. There are different interpretations of the meaning of the "magic charms" sown on their sleeves and the "veils" made for their heads. The King James Version uses some unusual imagery: "And say, Thus saith the Lord GOD; Woe to the women that sew pillows to all armholes, and make kerchiefs upon the head of every stature to hunt souls!" In his commentary regarding this verse, Adam Clarke says:

That sew pillows to all arm holes—I believe this refers to those cushions which are so copiously provided in the eastern countries for the apartments of women; on which they sit, lean, rest their heads, and prop up their arms. I have several drawings of eastern ladies, who are represented on sofas; and often with their arm thrown over a pillow, which is thereby pressed close to their side, and against which they thus recline. The prophet's discourse seems to point out that state of softness and effeminacy to which the predictions of those false prophetesses allured the inhabitants of Jerusalem. A careless voluptuous life is that which is here particularly reprehended.

And make kerchiefs—Probably some kind of ornamental dress which rendered women more enticing, so that they could the more successfully hunt or inveigle souls (men) into the worship of their false gods. These they put on heads of every stature—women of all ages, of every woman that rose up to inveigle men to idolatry.[4]

The NAS and NJKV translate Ezekiel 13:18 with a different, more mystical rendition of the text. They use "magic bands" and "magic charms" instead of "pillows for the sleeves," and "veils" instead of "kerchiefs." Warren Wiersbe says:

> The Jewish women Ezekiel was exposing were more like sorceresses who claimed to be prophetesses. They practiced the magical arts they had probably learned in Babylon, all of which were forbidden to the Jews. They manufactured magic charms that people could wear on various parts of the body and thus ward off evil. They also told fortunes and enticed people to buy their services. Like the false prophets, they were using the crisis situation for personal gain and preying on the fears of the people.[5]

What were the instructions given through Moses to the Israelites regarding the pagan customs that they would encounter in the Promised Land? See Deuteronomy 18:9-14 and record what you learn.

The wicked practices of the Israelite women were not something new in Ezekiel's day. The Lord had spoken against their practices many years before through Isaiah. Read Isaiah 3:16-26 and record how the women dressed, how they behaved, and how the Lord would judge them.

How wicked a woman can be! It is important for us to see what can happen when we do not fear the Lord.

Turn back to Ezekiel 13:20-23 now and read once again the judgment that the Lord announces that He will carry out against the practices of these women. Make note of who or what the Lord is against, and His ultimate goal.

"They shall know that I am the Lord." This was the deepest desire of our Lord God. It always was. It always will be. That we would be His people and that He would be our God. He keeps His Word and He fulfills His purposes. Let's look at a few Jewish women who did come to know that He is the Lord.

Look at the following passages and briefly describe the sincere relationship that these women experienced with the Lord and how it showed in their lives.

Matthew 26:6-13

Luke 8:1-3

Acts 9:36

How would you describe your relationship with the Lord? How would He describe you?

Please take time to consider your own words and actions in light of what we have studied today. Do you speak out of your own heart and spirit or do you speak the true Words of the Lord? Do you give the appearance of righteousness when inside all is decaying? Do you entice others to sin by the way you dress or behave? Do you turn to "false divination" for hope when you should turn to the true Word of God? Examine your heart and your mind and allow the Holy Spirit to convict, cleanse and encourage you.

He who would love life and see good days,

Let him refrain his tongue from evil, and his lips from speaking deceit.

Let him turn away from evil and do good. Let him seek peace and pursue it.

1 Peter 3:10-11

LESSON FOUR   *Hypocrites and Heroes*   **EZEKIEL 14**

I pray for you today, that any of you who have turned just slightly away from the face of the Lord will quickly turn back to see Him face to face.

יהוה

There have been periods of time in the history of Israel when the Lord has been silent. There have been times in my own life when it has seemed that the Lord was not speaking. Neither is the case in our study today! In this unit so far, we have seen the Lord speak to the whole house of Israel who were hard-of-hearing and hard-of-heart, we have seen the Lord speak to the false prophets and prophetesses, and today we will see what the Lord said through Ezekiel to the elders of the land. He even had something to say about true prophets and real heroes of the faith! Chapter 14 divides easily into two major sections:

    I. *"The Word of the Lord against False Religion" (Ezekiel 14:1-11)*

    II. *"The Word of the Lord against False Hope." (Ezekiel 14:12-23)*[6]

Please read Ezekiel 14:1-11 and note your observations below.

Who is mentioned in this passage?

Where does this take place?

What fraudulent actions are addressed?

The elders were setting up idols in their hearts unlike the worshippers at the temple who were worshipping the creatures on the wall. Women weeping for Tammuz, priests worshipping the sun, prophetesses doing witchcraft - these actions were public, but the Lord was addressing a hidden, heart issue. The elders appeared to be seeking the Lord by going to see Ezekiel, but God knew their hearts.

The specific sin of the elders is that "these men have set up their idols in their hearts, and put before them that which cause them to stumble into iniquity." (Ezekiel 14:3) This phrase is repeated in the first section of Chapter 14. Look at the other occurrences of this phrase in verses 3-11 and record the impact that the idolatry of the heart has on the peoples' relationship with the Lord.

Idolatry in the heart causes:

A stumbling block. An obstacle. A barrier. The word "stumbling block" in the Hebrew is "miksol" and according to the Keil and Delitzch commentary it means: "to allow anything to come into the mind, to permit it to rise up in the heart, to be mentally busy therewith." The same commentary also states that: "To set before one's face is also to be understood, in a spiritual sense, as relating to a thing which a man will not put out of his mind, a stumbling-block to sin and guilt, i.e., the idols. Thus the two phrases simply denote the leaning of the heart and spirit towards false gods."[7]

The definition of stumbling block given by Keil and Delitzch should prompt us to consider possible idols that we have set up in our own hearts. What do you allow to come into your mind that doesn't belong there? What do you allow yourself to become mentally busy with, consumed, or distracted by?

There are very clear tests for the things that we are to think on. We need to put roadblocks up to keep from letting stumbling blocks stack up in our hearts and minds.

What should not be allowed to enter your thoughts according to 2 Corinthians 10:5?

What are the right ways to think and thoughts to have based on the following verses?

Romans 12:3

Philippians 4:8

What are some practical things that you can do to think rightly and not allow any idols to be set up in your heart which would cause you to stumble?

The Lord's message through Ezekiel to the elders exiled in Babylon was one that was echoed through Paul to leaders in the early church. He told the Corinthians: "If anyone thinks himself to be a prophet or spiritual, let him acknowledge that the things which I write to you are the commandments of the Lord."

The Lord declared through Ezekiel that the elders would be held accountable for their actions. However, in the midst of many proclamations of imminent destruction, the Lord stretches out His hand with a gracious offer.

What did the Lord say to the house of Israel in Ezekiel 14:6?

Repent! Do you know what a wonderful word that is? It's a word that is full of grace and mercy! It's a word that gives hope. It was a word that the Lord repeated twice in this verse, sixty-two times in Ezekiel.

Please look at the full definition of this word:

Repent: Strong's #7725

Hebrew word:

Hebrew definition:

The offer and call to repent was spoken by the New Testament prophet John the Baptist as well as by Jesus and the apostles. Look at the references below and describe repentance according to these verses.

Luke 13:3

Acts 3:19

A final verse in Acts 8:22 summarizes the original message that the Lord communicated to the Israelites who had secretly cherished idols in their thoughts and hearts. What does it say?

Once again, the Lord expressed His ultimate desire to the elders and the whole house of Israel. It is crucial to remember this purpose as we study the confrontations, judgments, and seemingly merciless pronouncements made by the Lord.

What is the Lord's desire according to Ezekiel 14:8 and 11?

Can you see and hear and feel the love of the Lord God for His people? The book of Ezekiel doesn't come across as a warm and fuzzy love letter, but the love of the Lord is clearly spoken, even when it has to be in the language of tough love. Remember that the name of the Lord, YAHWEH, is one that expresses a personal relationship. Keep this in mind as we look at the second section of Chapter 14. Now we will hear the Word of the Lord spoken against false hope.

Please read Ezekiel 14:12-23.

In verse 13 we see that once again the Lord addresses "the land" of Israel and the judgment that will come about in it as a result of the unfaithfulness of the people.

The Word of the Lord given in this section of Chapter 14 is dramatically expressed. There are four refrains of possible conditions, crescendoing into a strong declaration at the end. Filling in the blanks below will help to highlight key words we observe and consider this scripture.

^{12}The word of the Lord came again to me, saying:

^{13} "Son of man, when a land sins _____ _____ by persistent _____, I will stretch out My hand _____ _____; I will cut off its _____ _____ _____, send _____ on it, and cut off man and beast from it. ^{14}Even if these three men, _____ _____, and _____ were in it, they would deliver _____ _____ by their righteousness," says the Lord GOD.

^{15} "If I cause _____ _____ to pass through the land, and they _____ it, and make it so _____ that no man may pass through because of the beasts,

^{16}even though _____ _____ _____ were in it, as I live," says the Lord GOD, "they would _____ _____ _____ _____ _____; only _____ would be delivered, and the land would be _____.

^{17} "Or if I _____ _____ _____ on that land, and say, '_____, go through the land,' and I cut off man and beast from it,

^{18}even though _____ _____ _____ were in it, as I live," says the

Lord GOD, "they would deliver _____ _____ _____ _____, but only _____ _____ would be delivered.

¹⁹ "Or if I send __ _____ into that land and pour out _____ _____ on it in blood, and cut off from it man and beast,

²⁰even though _____, _____ and _____ were in it, as I live," says the Lord GOD, "they would _____ neither son nor daughter; they would deliver _____ _____ by their _____."

²¹For thus says the Lord GOD:

"How much more it shall be when I send My four severe judgments on Jerusalem—the _____and _____ and _____ _____ and _____ — to cut off man and beast from it?"

The Lord described once again the four judgments that He would send on the people of Judah and Jerusalem. He has already proclaimed that these would come against the land and the people (Ezekiel 5:17), but the house of Israel continued to doubt His word. He repeated it to them here. Let us remember that God keeps His word.

Look at the following Scriptures and note the blessings and curses given in the Lord's covenant with His people.

Leviticus 26:9-26

Deuteronomy 32:21-25

What are your thoughts about the covenant that the Lord made with His people and the way that they responded to Him?

In the midst of describing His wrath to come, the Lord makes a surprising referral to three men from His Hall of Faith! Noah, Daniel, and Job had quite a reputation. Even the rebellious people exiled in Babylon would have known who they were.

Note how they are described in the following verses:

Noah: Genesis 6:8-9

Job: Job 1:1, 8; 2:3

Daniel: Daniel 1:4, 8

You probably know the stories of these men. Each of them was involved in interceding for or rescuing friends, family, and even animals. The Lord was making the point that even these righteous men who had already been servants of deliverance would not be able to deliver the house of Israel from the judgment of the Lord which was to come. Individuals would be held accountable for their actions. This crucial truth will be addressed again in Ezekiel 18.

Please read the last two verses of this chapter, Ezekiel 14:22-23 and then answer the following questions:

In spite of the destruction and death caused by the wrath of the Lord, what would be *brought out of the land*?

What would Ezekiel and the exiles *see*?

What impact would seeing this have on Ezekiel?

I must tell you that at first reading, these verses sound positive and encouraging. But actually, they aren't. The key to understanding what the Lord is communicating to Ezekiel is that the remnant being brought out of the destroyed land of Israel is a remnant of the unrighteous.

The Lord knew that Ezekiel was burdened for his people, his land, and his heritage. It was deeply distressing to already be in captivity, it was agonizing to continually proclaim the coming judgment of the Lord, and it was excruciatingly painful to actually watch the destruction of the people and the land. Ezekiel would have needed comfort, and the exiles that were with him would have longed for times of comfort and refreshment as well.

Write the Lord's statement to them in Ezekiel 14:23 :

"And they will comfort you, when you see their ways and their doings;

and you shall know _____

_____."

Can you accept the truth of the Lord even when it is painful? Can you accept the hand of the Lord and His ways even when they are distressing? We must know Who He is. We must know that He is holy. That He is sovereign. We must know that He is God and we are not.

Please look at the following verses and note what you learn about the reasons for the actions of our Almighty God.

Nehemiah 9:33

Jeremiah 22:8-9

Romans 2:5

Whatever you may be facing in your life at this time, please turn to the Lord and trust His ways. Whether you are facing discipline from your loving Father or a trial from your transforming Lord, or a time of refreshing and comfort from your gentle Shepherd, you can have peace by acknowledging the sovereignty of God.

There is no part of the conduct of God towards man that is not dictated by the purest principles of justice, equity, and truth. He does nothing but what is right; and whatever is right to be done, that ought to be done. In God's justice there is no severity; in God's mercy there is no caprice. He alone doth all things well; for he is the Fountain of justice and mercy.[8]   Adam Clarke

Reviewing the Revelations

Unit Four

The Truth is Told

Ezekiel 12—14

What were the most meaningful Scriptures or truths from this unit's lessons?

How do these truths impact your daily life?

Is there anything that you have questions about?

Prayer Requests and Praises

Today's Date:

My personal request:

Confidential requests from my friends:

If you abide in Me, and My words abide in you,
ask whatever you wish, and it shall be done for you. John 15:7 NASB

Notes

UNIT FIVE

Powerful Parables

LESSON ONE
The Worthless Vine
EZEKIEL 15

LESSON TWO
The Abandoned Baby
EZEKIEL 16:1-14

LESSON THREE
The Unfaithful Wife
EZEKIEL 16:15-63

LESSON FOUR
The Withering Vine and The Majestic Cedar
EZEKIEL 17

LESSON ONE   *The Worthless Vine*   EZEKIEL 15

Please pray that the Holy Spirit would teach you the Word of the Lord so that you may walk worthy of Him and be fruitful in every good work.

יהוה

I am overwhelmed with anticipation of what the Lord has in store for our study today and this unit! We will be studying Ezekiel 15, 16 and 17 which are chapters that speak to us through parables and images to express the heart of the Lord. I've looked ahead at these passages and I am deeply moved by the story that the Lord will tell us in Chapter 16. We'll have to dig deep into our contemplative cranium to grasp the message in Chapter 17. But oh, the impact that Chapter 15 will have on us! I'm so glad it's first! Once again we will see the unfaithfulness of the house of Israel, but then we will see the faithfulness of the Lord.

Please read Ezekiel 15.

How does the Lord describe "the wood of the vine" in verses 2-5?

How does the Lord compare the inhabitants of Jerusalem to the wood of the vine in verses 6 and 7?

What is the purpose for the Lord's actions according to verses 7 and 8?

The vine was a symbol of Israel. Turn to the following passages and record what you learn about the nation as described in these verses.

Psalm 80:8-18

Isaiah 5:1-7

Jeremiah 2:21

In our culture today, the image of a vineyard is a romantic one of sweeping hills, manicured rows of lush green leaves, branches dripping with large bunches of juicy grapes. California draws tourists into its fertile valleys to enjoy the beauty of their vineyards and the bounty of their produce. The vine planted by the Lord was supposed to bear good fruit, but it produced wild grapes instead, and they were sour grapes at that. The illustration given in Ezekiel 15 shows the barrenness and uselessness of the vine, Israel. It was good for nothing, except to be burned and cast aside.

The illustration of the vine in Ezekiel 15 prepares the way for the old to be cast aside and the new to be planted. When Israel failed to be a good vine, the Lord planted the true vine Who was and is faithful and bears much fruit. Rejoice with me as we look at another 15th chapter in the Bible, John 15:1-8.

> For He shall grow up before Him as a tender plant, and as a root out of dry ground.   Isaiah 53:2

Please read John 15:1-8 and savor the refreshment that comes from the True Vine. Record what you learn about each of the following:

Jesus

The Father

You

Fruit-bearing branches

Barren branches

Abiding

Please look up the definition of the following word:

Abide: Strong's #3306

Greek word:

Greek definition:

The nation of Israel was chosen by the Lord to bear fruit and glorify Him, but they were incapable of doing so. We too are chosen to bear fruit and we too are incapable of doing so. Jesus clearly said, "Apart from Me, you can do nothing." He is the true, good, healthy vine and we are branches attached to Him; as He lives through us He will bear fruit through us. The secret of the Vine is abiding.

One of my favorite saints is Andrew Murray (1828-1917) and his book, "The True Vine," is in the top-ten category of my favorite books. In it he says:

> *A branch is simply a bit of wood, brought forth by the vine for the one purpose of serving it in bearing fruit... The vine has its stores of life and sap and strength not for itself, but for the branches. The branches are and have nothing but what the vine provides and imparts. The believer is called to, and it is his highest blessedness to enter upon, a life of entire and unceasing dependence upon Christ. Day and night, every moment, Christ is to work in him all he needs.*[1]

Depending. Remaining. Staying close. Abiding. Relationship. That's what it's all about. That you may know the Lord.

Do you understand your position as a branch on the true vine? What does this mean to you?

Are you receiving life from the vine and bearing fruit? What kind of fruit?

The vineyard is cared for by the Vinedresser, the Father, and goes through different seasons and stages of growth. Consider the season that you are in at this time. If you are attached to the vine and abiding in Christ, then you can rest in the care of the Vinedresser.

LESSON TWO — The Abandoned Baby — EZEKIEL 16:1-15

Bow before your Lord today and ask Him to show you His unfailing love for you through His Word.

In this lesson and the next, we will study Ezekiel 16. It is a very long chapter covering the history of Israel and the love of the Lord for her in spite of her wayward, sinful, selfish lifestyle. I mentioned yesterday that I am deeply moved by the story that the Lord tells us in this chapter. I hope that you will see the heart of the Lord, the ever-faithful Husband, as you spend time absorbing His perspective of the life of His beloved. This chapter contains some graphic imagery, but the Word of the Lord is discreet in sensitive areas and we will consider these details with modesty and as delicately as possible. The story that we will read today begins with "once upon a time" and the end of the story one day will be "and they lived happily ever after." Please find a comfortable place to sit back and listen to the Lord tell you the story of His beloved as you read Ezekiel 16 in its entirety.

What is your initial response to the drama just unfolded before you?

Ezekiel 16 can be divided or outlined according to the stages of the story. Review the passages below and provide a theme or summary statement of what occurs in each of them. I've already entitled the five major divisions.

I. Her Beginning   Ezekiel 16:1-5 _____

                                                Ezekiel 16:6-7 _____

                                                Ezekiel 16:8 _____

                                                Ezekiel 16:9-14 _____

II. Her Unfaithfulness   Ezekiel 16:15-19 _____

                                                Ezekiel 16:20-22 _____

                                                Ezekiel 16:23-26 _____

                                                Ezekiel 16:27-30 _____

                                                Ezekiel 16:31-34 _____

III. Her Consequences   Ezekiel 16:35-41 _____

                                                Ezekiel 16:42-43 _____

IV. Her Repulsiveness   Ezekiel 16:44-52 _____

                                                Ezekiel 16:53-59 _____

V. Her Restoration   Ezekiel 16:60-63 _____

Now that we have surveyed this chapter and have an idea of what it is about, let's begin to look more closely at the details. Look at Ezekiel 16:1-3. "The Word of the Lord came to me" is how the story begins. What was the purpose of this particular message?

Please review and note the meaning for the word: **Abomination**, from page 56.

One of my resources says that the word abomination describes that which makes one physically ill. Can you imagine the emotion of the Lord as He tells this story?

As He held His grief in check, the Lord remembered the birth of Israel. According to Ezekiel 16:3-5, where did she come from, and how did He find her?

Determine Israel's ancestors according to the following verses:

Genesis 10:1, 6, 15 and Genesis 23:10-11, 17-20

The very land that Israel was given had belonged to the Amorites and Hittites. These two tribes were the most powerful of the Canaanite nations. They were "so abominably corrupt as to have been doomed to utter extermination by God."[2] (Leviticus 18:24-25, 28) The Lord pointed out that this mother and father were wicked pagans and that they had basically birthed Israel and abandoned her to die.

Verses 4-6 give a complete description of caring for a newborn baby according to traditional ancient eastern customs. What does the Lord say was *not* done for Israel?

"And when I passed by you and saw you struggling in your own blood, I said to you in your blood, 'Live!'" (Ezekiel 16:6) It was the Lord who cut, washed, rubbed with salt, swaddled and showed compassion upon Israel. The "struggle" is understood to mean the time of oppression of Israel under the rule of the Egyptians.

How did they struggle according to Exodus 1:11-14?

Ezekiel 16:7 shows the transformation that comes about in the life of one who belongs to the Lord and is nurtured by Him. The next passage refers to the Lord's "marriage" to Israel. We find the phrase "I spread My skirt over you" in Ezekiel 16:8 which is also found in Ruth 3:9. One of the ways that young women became engaged was when a suitor spread his garment or cloak or skirt over her. Covering with a skirt symbolized the protection and care that the wife would receive through her marriage.

We see the Lord repeat His wedding vow in this verse. What did He say?

The two key words in Ezekiel 16:8 are love and covenant. The verses below describe the love of the Lord for Israel. Look at the following verses and the meaning for love in each.

Deuteronomy 4:37

Love: Strong's #157

Hebrew word:

Hebrew definition:

Deuteronomy 7:7-8

Love: Strong's #2836

Hebrew word:

Hebrew definition:

What does this tell you about the love of the Lord for Israel?

Did the Lord choose Israel because it was worthy of love? No. What similarity do you see in the Lord's love for us?

What do you learn about the love of the Lord for us according to the following verses?

Romans 5:8

1 John 4:9

The covenant of the Lord may very well be the most important concept in the whole Bible. As with many of the truths that we are touching in the book of Ezekiel, we could spend weeks studying "covenant." We will barely scratch the surface today as we try to grasp the basics of the Lord's covenant with Israel. We will have more opportunities to consider covenant in later passages of Ezekiel.

The very first covenant was between the Lord and Noah. What were its terms and who had the burden of keeping the covenant? See Genesis 9:12-17.

The next covenant was between the Lord and Abram. What were its terms? See Genesis 15:12-21 and Genesis 17:1-10.

The covenant that the Lord referred to in Ezekiel 16:8 is the one that He made with the Israelites after delivering them from Egypt. It was given through Moses at Mount Sinai and is covered in detail in chapters 20 through 23 of Exodus, with the most familiar aspect of this covenant being the Ten Commandments. There were were actually many more than ten commandments given!

What did the Lord promise, what did He require, and how did the people respond? See Exodus 19:3-8.

"And you became Mine, says the Lord." (Ezekiel 16:8) Remember that the Lord is telling the story of His relationship with His beloved. How is the response of Israel to the Lord at the time of the Mosaic covenant described in the following verses?

Exodus 24:3-7

Jeremiah 2:2

Let's review the story up to this point and then consider the wedding gifts bestowed upon Israel following the Lord's betrothal to her with His covenant.

Please read Ezekiel 16:1-14.

What were the blessings that Israel received because of the Lord's covenant with her? List the actions of the Lord as well as His provisions according to Ezekiel 16:9-14.

> As long as Israel, Jehovah's wife, obeyed His word and kept His covenant, He blessed her abundantly just as He promised. He gave her healthy children, fruitful flocks and herds, abundant harvests, and protection from disease, disaster, and invasion. There wasn't one word of the covenant that the Lord failed to keep, and the reputation of Israel spread far and wide. During Solomon's day, foreign rulers came to listen to him.[3]

How would you summarize the story of the Lord and His beloved Israel up to this point?

From our vantage point in history, we can see how the Lord made something out of nothing. He loved the unlovely. From sickness to health. From rags to riches. From poverty to privilege. He pledged His oath. He made His vow. He would not break His covenant with His beloved Israel. We too are covenanted to this same Lord, and we have been blessed with every spiritual blessing in Christ. Our lives have been changed as dramatically as was Israel's.

Look at the following verses which parallel Israel's story and note what the Lord did for you.

"...but you were thrown out into the open field, when you yourself were loathed on the day you were born." (Ezekiel 16:5)

Ephesians 2:12-13

Colossians 1:21-23

"And when I passed by you and saw you struggling in your own blood, I said to you in your blood, 'Live!'" (Ezekiel 16:6)

Ephesians 2:4-6

Colossian 2:13-15

"I swore an oath to you and entered into a covenant with you and you became Mine, says the Lord." (Ezekiel 16:8)

Ephesians 1:13-14

Colossians 3:3, 4

"I washed you in water; yes, I thoroughly washed off your blood, and I anointed you with oil." (Ezekiel 16:9)

Ephesians 5:25-27

"...your clothing was of fine linen, silk, and embroidered cloth." (Ezekiel 16:13)

Ephesians 4:20-24

Revelation 19:8

"...you were exceedingly beautiful and succeeded to royalty." (Ezekiel 16:13)

Ephesians 1:11

Colossians 2:9-10

This is your story if you have trusted in Jesus Christ as your Savior. You were loved when you were unlovable. What is your response to the Lord regarding His love for you?

We have already observed in Ezekiel 16 that Israel behaved as an unfaithful wife. Tomorrow we will consider her infidelity and its consequences and reflect on the warning that we receive for our own lives. Our Lord is a covenant-keeping God even when His people are not. Close today by praising the Lord for Who He is.

LESSON THREE   *The Unfaithful Wife*   EZEKIEL 16:15-63

May the Word of the Lord today help us draw closer in love and loyalty to Him. Pray that it will do so.

יהוה

As we have already seen often in our study of the book of Ezekiel, we will see again today in Ezekiel 16:15-63 the sins of Israel enumerated and the consequences thereof explained. Our previous study ended when Israel was exceedingly beautiful, and her fame went out among the nations. Her beauty was perfect through the splendor of the Lord which He bestowed upon her. How incredible! Perfect beauty! She was admired by the world. And then . . .

Please read Ezekiel 16:15-34. The word most repeated in this section is "harlot." Mark each occurrence of this word and list what you learn about Israel's harlotry.

Please look up the meaning of the word.

Harlot: Strong's #2181

Hebrew word:

Hebrew definition:

Ezekiel was given the responsibility for delivering to the exiled elders of Israel a message regarding Israel's unfaithfulness.

Read the comments below and record the details of Israel's history according to the verses given.

The people's unfaithfulness to God consisted of:[4]

1 – Building altars to idols and decorating the high places with their garments

1 Kings 11:7-8

2 – Fashioning male images (phallic or sexually perverse statues) from the gold and silver that God had provided

2 Chronicles 28:24

111

3 – Giving what belonged to the true God to these false gods

Isaiah 57:8

4 – Practicing human sacrifice to appease these gods

2 Kings 16:1-4

5 – Seeking political alliances with other nations instead of relying on the Lord for her security

Jeremiah 2:18, 19

What had caused Israel to become a brazen harlot, an adulterous wife? Pride and ingratitude. She had been warned of these dangerous sins even in her covenant with the Lord.

Record the pledge of devotion required in Deuteronomy 6:4-6 and the warning regarding infidelity found in Deuteronomy 6:10-15.

Could we also turn from our blessings and become brazenly sinful? I think I can hear you saying yes. Have we been given warnings as Israel was? I hear you . . . yes. But what are those warnings? We don't memorize them as our favorite verses. Let's look at a few of them now and take some time to soberly examine our hearts.

Record the warnings of the following Scriptures:

2 Corinthians 11:2-4

Colossians 2:8

James 4:4-6

Each of us have tendencies toward certain areas of weakness. To which of the weaknesses warned of in the verses above are you more susceptible? If you are struggling with something in particular at this time, take action now. Turn to the Lord, cry out for help, and make yourself accountable to someone whom you can trust.

"Woe, woe to you!" said the Lord to Israel, his unfaithful wife. "Now then, O harlot, hear the Word of the Lord!"

Read Ezekiel 16:35-43. According to this passage, how would the Lord recompense Israel for her wicked deeds?

What do you learn about the Lord from Ezekiel 16:41-42?

The next characters in the story of Israel remind me of the two terrible step-sisters in "Cinderella." Unfortunately, Israel was not the sweet little girl that Cinderella was, but was terribly more wicked than her sisters.

Read Ezekiel 16:44-59.

How is Samaria described?

How is Sodom described?

Note what you learn about the background of Samaria according to 1 Kings 16:29-33.

What do you learn about Sodom according to Genesis 13:10-13?

Summarize how Israel is described in Ezekiel 16:44-58 compared to Samaria and Sodom.

The justice of the sovereign, holy Lord is evident again in Ezekiel 16:59. What did the Lord say He would do?

"Nevertheless." (Ezekiel 16:60) What an incredible word. What a word of mercy and grace. What a word of promise and hope. What does the Lord say He will do in Ezekiel 16:60-63?

Look up the meaning for the following word:

Everlasting: Strong's #5769

Hebrew word:

Hebrew definition:

Even though Israel had broken their covenant with the Lord, He promised that He would make a new covenant with them. This prophecy remains to be fulfilled. But as certain as judgment was, so certain is this promise.

Note what Israel will receive in her everlasting covenant from the following verses:

Isaiah 45:17

Isaiah 51:11

Jeremiah 32:40

And they will live happily ever after. The story of the Lord and His beloved Israel comes to a close. The future of the beloved nation is bright and wonderful, even though her past is tainted. The same is true for you.

> When the kindness and the love of God our Savior toward man appeared, not by works of righteousness which we have done, but according to His mercy He saved us, through the washing of regeneration and renewing of the Holy Spirit, whom He poured out on us abundantly through Jesus Christ our Savior, that having been justified by His grace we should become heirs according to the hope of eternal life.
> Titus 3:4-7

LESSON FOUR The Withered Vine and The Majestic Cedar EZEKIEL 17

Pause to pray that the Holy Spirit will give you wisdom to understand the Lord's purpose in His written record of Israel.

𐤉𐤅𐤄𐤅

We have had two days of being immersed in the history of Israel. Please keep in mind the truth of the following verse as you reflect on what we have studied and as you prepare to study the riddle posed by the Lord in Ezekiel 17.

What will you gain from studying even the most obscure passages of the Bible? Please apply Romans 15:4 to your answer.

It is probable that the exiled elders of Israel were unmoved by the Lord's analogy of His nation as a wild, unfruitful vine, and unresponsive to His story of Israel as His adulterous wife. Perhaps the Word of the Lord that we will study today was an attempt to stimulate the dull hearts and minds of the Israelites with a brainteaser. I think at first we will find it quite puzzling and then intriguing as we discover the explanation of it.

Please read Ezekiel 17:1-10.

There are three characters to examine in this riddle. Please list their descriptions below.

A great eagle (v.3)

The vine

Another great eagle

The characters are the two eagles and the vine, and the actual question posed by the Lord in the riddle is "Will it (the vine) thrive?" What message seems to be being communicated in this question? See Ezekiel 17:9, 10.

The key to solving this riddle is just to read a little further! Obviously the Lord did not intend for Ezekiel's audience to have any doubt regarding the explanation of the parable.

Please read Ezekiel 17:11-21.

The riddle is unraveled by matching the symbolic elements to the real-life characters. Look at the historical accounts in 2 Kings 24:8-17, 2 Chronicles 36:9-14 and Jeremiah 37:5-7, then review the explanation from the Lord in Ezekiel 17:11-21. You will probably also want to look at a commentary to determine the explanation of the following:

The great eagle (v.3)

Lebanon (v.3)

The topmost young twig

The land of trade

The seed

The fertile field

Another great eagle

The vine

What is the point of this riddle and its interpretation? What did the Lord want to communicate to the Israelites? Make sure you notice the repetition of the word "covenant" in this chapter.

I must admit that even though the riddle is intriguing and I do enjoy puzzles, I feel like the message that the Lord has conveyed in this chapter is old news. But wait! We haven't read or studied the complete Word of the Lord in this chapter! There is big news in the next few verses! Hang in there. Persevere with me through a little bit more symbolism.

Please read Ezekiel 17:22-24, quoted below. Underline what the Lord says He will do. Highlight what the Lord is going to plant and what it will become.

Ezekiel 17:22-24 ²²Thus says the Lord GOD: "I will take also one of the highest branches of the high cedar and set it out. I will crop off from the topmost of its young twigs a tender one, and will plant it on a high and prominent mountain. ²³On the mountain height of Israel I will plant it; and it will bring forth boughs, and bear fruit, and be a majestic cedar. Under it will dwell birds of every sort; in the shadow of its branches they will dwell. ²⁴And all the trees of the field shall know that I, the LORD, have brought down the high tree and exalted the low tree, dried up the green tree and made the dry tree flourish; I, the LORD, have spoken and have done it."

In the first riddle, King Jehoiachin was the highest shoot or branch in King David's family tree and he was planted in Babylon by Nebuchadnezzar. King Zedekiah was the seed that was planted in the fertile field of Israel by Nebuchadnezzar and grew into a spindly vine instead of a stately tree. He was the last king in Israel and saw his sons killed before his eyes. When he died in Babylon it seemed that the Davidic line had come to an end. This was not the case and the last words of the Lord in Ezekiel 17 were His words of hope for a future king from David's family as He had promised.

That king would be none other than Jesus!

Let's look at this passage now in light of this. Jesus is the tender one.

What do you learn about His coming reign from the following verses?

Isaiah 11:1

Jeremiah 23:5-6

Zechariah 6:12-13

Jesus Christ will return to the earth to reign as King of Israel one day in the future. But He is already on the throne! He is already King of Kings!

Please see this for yourself in these passages and describe what you observe.

Ephesians 1:20-21

Hebrews 12:2

"Blessing and honor and glory and power be to Him who sits on the throne, and to the Lamb, forever and ever!" Yes, Jesus Christ is King. He is on the throne in heaven and will be on the throne on earth one day. But is He on the throne in your own life? Or are you on the throne? Is there evidence in your life that you are submitting to His reign?

There shall be a root of Jesse; and He that shall rise to reign over the Gentiles, in Him shall the Gentiles trust."   Romans 15:12 KJV

Reviewing the Revelations

Unit Five

Powerful Parables

Ezekiel 15—17

What were the most meaningful Scriptures or truths from this unit's lessons?

How do these truths impact your daily life?

Is there anything that you have questions about?

Prayer Requests and Praises

Today's Date:

My personal request:

Confidential requests from my friends:

You help us by your prayers.

2 Corinthians 1:11 NIV

Notes

UNIT SIX
Proclaiming the Prophecy

LESSON ONE
Announcing Accountability
EZEKIEL 18

LESSON TWO
Lamenting the Leadership
EZEKIEL 19

LESSON THREE
Remembering the Past
EZEKIEL 20

LESSON FOUR
Sounding the Alarm
EZEKIEL 21

LESSON ONE *Announcing Accountability* EZEKIEL 18

Get down on your knees and pray. It won't take but a moment into your study to realize that the truths of this chapter are hard to grasp.

יהוה

Our Lord wants us to know Him and His ways. Let's give Him our full attention as we study Ezekiel 18. The past few chapters were creative dissertations on the state of the nation. Now the Word of the Lord is going to get very personal.

Please read Ezekiel 18:1-3.

What did the Lord tell the people to stop saying?

The main idea of this proverb was that children are impacted and affected by their parents' choices. This "proverb" was not a wise saying, but actually a statement made to excuse one's personal responsibility. Basically, it meant: "It's not my fault! It's my family's fault!" The blame game has been very popular ever since Adam started playing it in the garden of Eden.

The rest of chapter 18 is a lesson from the Lord in individual accountability. Ezekiel had to remind the people that experiencing hardship as a consequence of the sins of ancestors was not the same as judgment for one's own sins.[1]

What does the Lord say about individuals in Ezekiel 18:4?

Please describe the scenarios given in the following passages:

Ezekiel 18:5-9 – "The righteous man"

Ezekiel 18:10-13 – "The wicked son"

Ezekiel 18:14-20 – "The righteous grandson"

Ezekiel 18:21-23 – "The wicked man repenting"

Ezekiel 18:24 – "The righteous man revolting"

There are statements of truth in these passages that probably make you uncomfortable to say the least. Does this passage base salvation on a man's works? Does this passage teach that one can lose their salvation? No and no! Keep in mind that we study the truths of Scripture according to the cultural times and according to the context of the whole of Scripture.

The explanations given here were for the Jews who had made a covenant with the Lord. The covenant clearly explained that obedience brought blessing and that disobedience brought punishment.

What did the Lord say in His covenant in Exodus 20:5,6? It is very important to notice how the later generations are described in both of these verses.

And what did the Lord teach through Moses in Deuteronomy 24:16?

Hopefully looking at those verses together show you that an individual is responsible for his own actions. Now let's consider the possibility that a person can be saved by his works, as may seem to be implied in Ezekiel 18:5-9 and Ezekiel 18:21-23. First, turn to Ephesians 2:8,9 and record what you learn.

Now look at Romans 4:3 and note what Abraham received and why he received it.

Continue to Romans 4:16 and fill in the following blanks:

"Therefore it is of _____ that it might be according to _____"

The saints of the Old Testament had faith in the Lord and His promise of salvation through the Messiah. Their faith was demonstrated by their actions, or their works, just as today our faith should be seen by our good works. But salvation is and was and always will be dependent on the grace of God in Christ Jesus.

There is one other issue that I mentioned previously that probably comes to mind when reading Ezekiel 18:24. Can a righteous man turn from the Lord and lose his salvation? Ezekiel was not referring to what we call "the security of the believer," because he was not referring to eternal life or eternal death in this passage. He was referring to physical death as punishment for unrighteousness. While Ezekiel was presenting hypothetical situations, he did have real history to draw upon. There were righteous men in the Old Testament who died when they turned away from the Lord.

Take a few minutes and read the story of the "man of God" who delivered the prophetic Word of the Lord to King Jeroboam, but disobeyed the Lord on his return home. Read 1 Kings 13:21-26. Record what happened to the man of God and why it happened.

The man of God experienced the reality that the Lord keeps His word, which was what Ezekiel was communicating to the Israelites. What did they say in return to him, according to Ezekiel 18:25 and 29?

The Israelites wanted the Lord to bless them for obedience, but wanted Him to turn the other way for their disobedience. The Lord wanted turning, but He wanted it from the Israelites. How did He instruct them and give them hope in Ezekiel 18:30-32?

The Lord was communicating His heart through Ezekiel. He was directing and motivating the nation of Israel to seek Him for a new heart. "Get yourselves a new heart and a new spirit." Their response, if they were listening, would have to have been – how can I get a new heart? How can I get a new spirit? Nicodemus is a good example of a devout Israelite who came up against the same questions. Jesus had the answer then, and the answer is still the same today: You must be born again. (John 3:1-16)

Read Ezekiel 18:1-24 and consider the five scenarios which illustrate an individual's personal accountability toward God. You could be living out any one of those scenarios. Which one best describes you today?

If you have been saved by grace and are exhibiting your faith and righteousness through good works, then press on, but heed the warning that disobedience brings discipline. If you have not trusted Jesus Christ as your Savior, or if you are behaving in disobedience to Him, respond to the Lord's instructions in Ezekiel 18:30-32: "Repent, and turn from all your transgressions, so that iniquity will not be your ruin." Jesus died to forgive you of all of your sins. You get a new heart and a new spirit when you believe in Him.

DAY TWO   *Lamenting the Leadership*   EZEKIEL 19

Pray for patience and perseverance in your study today. The language and literature of Scripture is beautiful, but often sounds foreign to us.

הוהי

"Take up a lamentation for the princes of Israel." This was the Word of the Lord to Ezekiel as recorded in Ezekiel 19:1. Today's lesson will focus on the Lord's poem of lamentation.

Look up the definition for the following word:

Lamentation: Strong's #7015
Hebrew word:
Hebrew definition:

When would a poem or song of lamentation normally be sung?

Remember that Ezekiel was speaking to an audience in exile. They had been deported from their homeland of Israel. When they had last seen their beloved country, it was still being ruled by an Israelite king; the homes, villages, and city walls were still standing; and the temple was their national landmark. The lamentation now being presented to the exiles was a prophecy of the coming death and destruction of everything in the land of Israel.

According to Ezekiel 19:1, for whom was this lamentation written?

These were the leaders of the people. We will see that two specific kings are referred to in the lamentation: the first cub of the lioness was Jehoahaz and the other cub was Jehoiachin.

Please read Ezekiel 19:1-4 and note the details given regarding the young lion in this passage, then compare the description to that given of Jehoahaz in 2 Kings 23:31-344.

EZEKIEL 19:1-4	2 KINGS 23:31-34

And now please repeat the exercise for Ezekiel 19:5-9, noting the details given for the second young lion, and compare them to the description given of Jehoiachin in 2 Kings 24:8-10.

EZEKIEL 19:5-9	2 KINGS 24:8-12

Do you feel somewhat familiar with the stories of these kings who were taken into captivity? We have looked at these events previously in our studies. These two kings, Jehoahaz and Jehoiachin, would have been well-known to the exiles. Many of the exiles were still in Israel during the reign of Jehoahaz, and the first group of captives were brought to Babylon when Jehoiachin was taken captive. These powerful kings were captured by other kings and this lamentation was a reminder of that fact. If the kings could be captured by other nations, then the country of Israel could also be conquered by other nations, which was the prophecy that the Lord continued to reveal to the exiles.

This lamentation was not one that was full of grief for King Jehoahaz or King Jehoachin. Instead it was a statement of accusation against them for their rebellion against the will of God. These kings were the leaders of the people, but their leadership was not in submission to the Lord.

Stop and think for a moment about the leaders in your life. Who are your heroes? Who are your mentors? Are you following someone who is following the Lord?

The lamentation continues in Ezekiel 19:10-14. The vine refers once again, as it did in Ezekiel 15, to Israel. Her past and her present are described here. Record the description below.

ISRAEL'S PAST (v.10-11)	ISRAEL'S PRESENT (v.12-14)

There was a point in time during the reign of King David and during the early reign of King Solomon that Israel was — as the Lord described it through Ezekiel — fruitful, with strong branches, and towering in stature above thick branches.

Note the description of Israel according to 1 Kings 4:20-21.

The true mourning of the Lord and His lamentation is felt at the end of the poem in verses 13 and 14. The remnant of Israel is in exile in a foreign land and the nation has "no strong branch — no scepter for ruling."

Hosea prophesied 150 years before Ezekiel that this would occur. Look at Hosea 10:3 and record what the Israelites say.

But there is still hope for the people of Israel. The Lord is faithful and keeps His Word. What promise was given in Genesis 49:10 and in Numbers 24:17?

Please find the definition for the following word:
Scepter: Strong's #7626
Hebrew word:
Hebrew definition:

Last week we looked at several prophecies concerning the Branch of Righteousness that would be raised up in the line of David to be King. His birth was announce in Luke 1:31-33. Please record His name and how He is described.

The King was born! But the Israelites didn't recognize Him. Look at John 19:13-15 and record who said what regarding kings.

Even though the Israelites didn't recognize Jesus as their King, it didn't change the truth that He was and is the King of Kings. God the Father has declared it. What did He say about His Son in Hebrews 1:8?

The two young lions in Ezekiel 19 wore the crown of the King of Israel, but hated righteousness and loved lawlessness, therefore they were anointed with captivity and mourning. We know that Jesus Christ reigns today as the King of Kings, and He reigns with a scepter of righteousness. There will never be a song of lamentation and mourning for the end of His reign because His Kingdom will never end.

If you have been following the wrong king, you can change your allegiance today.

| LESSON THREE | *Remembering the Past* | EZEKIEL 20 |

Be still and know that He is God. Pray that the Holy Spirit will give you wisdom and revelation to know the Lord in His faithfulness, love, patience, and power today.

יהוה

In one chapter, the Lord gives a concise history of the nation of Israel and her rebellion against Him. Ezekiel 20 summarizes in 44 verses what is described through the books of Exodus, Numbers, Joshua, Judges, 1 and 2 Samuel, and 1 and 2 Kings. It will be a long chapter to study, but it will be a short study compared to reading or studying the history described in the books just mentioned!

Throughout our study so far of the book of Ezekiel, we have turned back to other Scriptures to see the first mention of the Lord's covenant and commands to His chosen people. Today, we will spend most of our time right in Ezekiel 20.

Would you please find a comfortable spot and just read Ezekiel 20:1-44? As you read, watch for the character of the Lord as well as the behavior of the Israelites.

What is your initial reaction to this "national review?" Did anything surprise you?

The time, place and recipients of this Word of the Lord is given in Ezekiel 20:1-4.

What was the date?

Who came to Ezekiel?

What was their request?

What was the purpose of this Word of the Lord?

The last mention of a date was in Ezekiel 8:1, which stated that Ezekiel was in his house on the fifth day of the month, in the sixth month, in the sixth year (of his captivity), and received the Word of the Lord at that time. The date given in Ezekiel 20:1 is approximately eleven months later, according to the scholars who can understand the various ancient calendars of the times! According to the Thomas Nelson Study Bible footnotes, this new date was at a point in time when King Zedekiah, on the throne in Jerusalem, made an alignment with Egypt against Babylon in hopes of deliverance from Nebuchadnezzar's attacks. It seems that the elders who came to Ezekiel wanted a divine explanation of the current events.[2] The Lord gave them an explanation, but it wasn't what they wanted to hear.

Read through Ezekiel 20:5-29 and highlight with one color the *actions of the Lord*, and highlight with another color the *response of the Israelites*. With a third color, highlight the Lord's ultimate purpose at all times: *that you may know the Lord.*

⁵"Say to them, 'Thus says the Lord GOD: "On the day when I chose Israel and raised My hand in an oath to the descendants of the house of Jacob, and made Myself known to them in the land of Egypt, I raised My hand in an oath to them, saying, 'I am the LORD your God.' ⁶On that day I raised My hand in an oath to them, to bring them out of the land of Egypt into a land that I had searched out for them, 'flowing with milk and honey,' the glory of all lands. ⁷Then I said to them, 'Each of you, throw away the abominations which are before his eyes, and do not defile yourselves with the idols of Egypt. I am the LORD your God.' ⁸But they rebelled against Me and would not obey Me. They did not all cast away the abominations which were before their eyes, nor did they forsake the idols of Egypt. Then I

said, 'I will pour out My fury on them and fulfill My anger against them in the midst of the land of Egypt.' ⁹But I acted for My name's sake, that it should not be profaned before the Gentiles among whom they were, in whose sight I had made Myself known to them, to bring them out of the land of Egypt.

¹⁰"Therefore I made them go out of the land of Egypt and brought them into the wilderness. ¹¹And I gave them My statutes and showed them My judgments, 'which, if a man does, he shall live by them.' ¹²Moreover I also gave them My Sabbaths, to be a sign between them and Me, that they might know that I am the LORD who sanctifies them. ¹³Yet the house of Israel rebelled against Me in the wilderness; they did not walk in My statutes; they despised My judgments, 'which, if a man does, he shall live by them;' and they greatly defiled My Sabbaths. Then I said I would pour out My fury on them in the wilderness, to consume them. ¹⁴But I acted for My name's sake, that it should not be profaned before the Gentiles, in whose sight I had brought them out. ¹⁵So I also raised My hand in an oath to them in the wilderness, that I would not bring them into the land which I had given them, 'flowing with milk and honey,' the glory of all lands, ¹⁶because they despised My judgments and did not walk in My statutes, but profaned My Sabbaths; for their heart went after their idols. ¹⁷Nevertheless My eye spared them from destruction. I did not make an end of them in the wilderness.

¹⁸"But I said to their children in the wilderness, 'Do not walk in the statutes of your fathers, nor observe their judgments, nor defile yourselves with their idols. ¹⁹I am the LORD your God: Walk in My statutes, keep My judgments, and do them; ²⁰hallow My Sabbaths, and they will be a sign between Me and you, that you may know that I am the LORD your God.'

²¹"Notwithstanding, the children rebelled against Me; they did not walk in My statutes, and were not careful to observe My judgments, 'which, if a man does, he shall live by them;' but they profaned My Sabbaths. Then I said I would pour out My fury on them and fulfill My anger against them in the wilderness. ²²Nevertheless I withdrew My hand and acted for My name's sake, that it should not be profaned in the sight of the Gentiles, in whose sight I had brought them out. ²³Also I raised My hand in an oath to those in the wilderness, that I would scatter them among the Gentiles and disperse them throughout the countries,

²⁴because they had not executed My judgments, but had despised My statutes, profaned My Sabbaths, and their eyes were fixed on their fathers' idols.

²⁵"'Therefore I also gave them up to statutes that were not good, and judgments by which they could not live; ²⁶and I pronounced them unclean because of their ritual gifts, in that they caused all their firstborn to pass through the fire, that I might make them desolate and that they might know that I am the LORD"

²⁷ "Therefore, son of man, speak to the house of Israel, and say to them, 'Thus says the Lord GOD: "In this too your fathers have blasphemed Me, by being unfaithful to Me. ²⁸When I brought them into the land concerning which I had raised My hand in an oath to give them, and they saw all the high hills and all the thick trees, there they offered their sacrifices and provoked Me with their offerings. There they also sent up their sweet aroma and poured out their drink offerings. ²⁹Then I said to them, 'What is this high place to which you go?' So its name is called Bamah to this day."'

How would you summarize the Lord's actions toward the nation of Israel?

How would you summarize the people's reaction to the Lord?

Are there any parallels to these observations in your own life?

The Lord gave the history of the nation of Israel because He knew there were parallels in the lives of the Israelites at the time of the exile. He spoke through Ezekiel to confront the elders with the rebellion of the people which was identical to the rebellion of their fathers.

What sins are the people confronted with in Ezekiel 20:29-32?

What actions does the Lord declare that He will take in Ezekiel 20:33-44?

The Lord made His purposes completely clear in verses 38 and 41-44. What were they?

Look up the definition for the following word:

Know: Strong's #3045

Hebrew word:

Hebrew definition:

Do you know the Lord? Take time now to praise Him for Who He is.

LESSON FOUR   *Sounding the Alarm*   EZEKIEL 20:45-21:32

Please pray that the Lord will open your eyes to see His sovereignty, His justice, and His promise for the future.

ヨイヨא

In the Hebrew Scriptures, Ezekiel 21 begins at what is now noted in our Bibles as Ezekiel 20:45. The five verses at the end of chapter 20 are a preliminary setting to chapter 21. We will look at it very briefly to see the relationship between Ezekiel 20:45-49 and Ezekiel 21:1-4.

Please read Ezekiel 20:45-49 and fill in the blanks below.

". . . say to the forest of the _____,

'Hear the Word of the Lord! Thus says the Lord GOD:

   "Behold, I will kindle a _____ in you,

and it shall devour every _____ tree and every _____ tree in you….."

Now read Ezekiel 21:1-4 and note the parallels with the previous verses.

"and say to the _____ _____ _____,

  'Thus says the LORD: "Behold, I am against you,

and I will draw ____ _____ out of its sheath

and cut off both _____ and _____ from you."

The key word in this chapter is "sword." The main point that the Lord is communicating regarding this weapon of judgment and justice is expressed in poetry in verses 9-11. Describe the specific details given about the sword from these verses.

The one who carries this sword as an agent of the Lord is described in Ezekiel 21:19-22. These verses refer to the King of Babylon, Nebuchadnezzar. This shouldn't come as a surprise to you! In many previous passages we have seen the actions and attack of Nebuchadnezzar prophesied.

What specific details about his attack are described in Ezekiel 21:19-22?

The following paragraph from John MacArthur's study notes on this passage will be helpful in gaining a further understanding of what the Lord prophesies that Nebuchadnezzar will do on his way to attack Jerusalem.

> **the king … stands … to use divination.** This means to "seek an omen," to gain guidance from superstitious devices (cf. Is. 47:8–15). Three methods are available to Babylon's leader. He shook arrows and let them fall, then read a conclusion from the pattern. He looked at Teraphim (idols), and examined an animal liver to gain help from his gods.[3]

While the account of Nebuchadnezzar's superstitious actions is not recorded in the Scriptures, history itself agrees with the truth of the Word of the Lord. Nebuchadnezzar first attacked Jerusalem according to the direction he received from his oracles, then turned to attack Ammon. (Ezekiel 21:22,28)

Was Nebuchadnezzar guided by the acts of divination or the hand of the Lord? What are your thoughts?

What do you learn regarding divination from the following verses?

Numbers 23:23

Deuteronomy 18:10

The nation of Israel was clearly not to use divination, sorcery, or witchcraft for any reason; but consulting something or someone other than the Lord has been a common practice from the earliest days of mankind. The Lord is not helpless against the spiritual wickedness involved in occultic activities; instead, He is completely able to control the outcome of such divinations to suit His sovereign will.

We believers are to seek the Lord and His will, and He has already provided answers to our questions through His written word. "A sword! A sword sharpened and also polished!" When the Israelites didn't obey the Word of the Lord, He used a sword to punish, correct, and lead them to repentance. He also uses a sword in our lives today.

What do you learn about the sword of the Lord from the following verses?

Ephesians 6:17

Hebrews 4:12

The sword of the Lord, whether wielded as a weapon of slaughter or as an instrument of instruction, is ultimately for the good of man and the glory of the Lord.

This chapter of the book of Ezekiel dramatically describes the coming slaughter of the Israelites through the sword of Nebuchadnezzar. It also describes the judgment that the country of Ammon will receive through the sword of Nebuchadnezzar because it sided with Babylon against Israel. And in this chapter, Ezekiel himself is commanded to react dramatically to the prophecy.

Read Ezekiel 21:1-7.

Fill in the blanks below to complete the statements from the Lord to Ezekiel:

_____, therefore, son of man, with a _____ _____

and _____ with _____ before their eyes.

Look up the definition for the following words:

Sigh: Strong's #584
Hebrew word:
Hebrew definition:

Breaking: Strong's #7670
Hebrew word:
Hebrew definition:

Bitterness: Strong's #4814
Hebrew word:
Hebrew definition:

Using your imagination, describe how this "thirty-something" year old priest-prophet might have carried out the command given to him by the Lord.

According to Ezekiel 21:7, what was Ezekiel to anticipate the reaction of the people to be when they saw him grieving?

And what response was Ezekiel to give to the people according to Ezekiel 21:7? Look closely at this verse for repeated adjectives. The Hebrew word kole, Strong's #3605, was repeated four times, but our translations have added some variety by using 2 different words for it.

The Lord further instructs Ezekiel to express his grief visibly in verses 12 and 14. What else is he commanded to do?

Jeremiah demonstrated a similar expression of grief. Look at Jeremiah 31:19 and note what he did, and why he did it.

Both Ezekiel and Jeremiah expressed extreme grief — Ezekiel on behalf of the destruction coming to Israel and Jeremiah on behalf of the sins of Israel. There was a time when Israel could have repented with grief for her sins and could have turned to the Lord, and could have been restored to Him. But she did not.

Throughout this book of prophecy, we have seen the foretelling of certain judgment on the people of Israel because of their disobedience to the Lord. The judgment of the Lord would cause the people to repent, to know the Lord as their God and to have a personal relationship with Him. The same call is given to us today, for the times when we have strayed from the way of the Lord.

According to James 4:7-10, what are we to do when we have fallen out of fellowship with the Lord?

Is there something in your life that is difficult and causing you grief right now? Your grief may not be due to repentance but instead due to rebellion. Please take a moment and pray through the verses in James that you have just read and draw near to the Lord. He is your hope.

The Lord demonstrated His kindness through Ezekiel by offering words of hope in the midst of His announcements of judgment. There is a little phrase in Chapter 21 that once again reminds the Israelites of the Lord's plan for the future. Fill in the blanks below by looking at Ezekiel 21:27.

"It shall be no longer, until _____ _____ whose _____ it is; and I will give it to _____."

Now that the specific prophecy regarding the Messiah has been highlighted for you, please read Ezekiel 21:25-27 and note what is being taken away from whom and what is being given to whom.

Look at Isaiah 9:6 for a more familiar prophecy which parallels that given in Ezekiel. What is being given to whom?

We have studied this chapter in bits and pieces, and we have taken it apart and looked at its history, its emotion, and its prophecy. Please read Ezekiel 21 in its entirety now and record the impact that this Word of the Lord has had on you today.

Reviewing the Revelations

Unit Six

Proclaiming the Prophecy

Ezekiel 18—21:32

What were the most meaningful Scriptures or truths from this unit's lessons?

How do these truths impact your daily life?

Is there anything that you have questions about?

Prayer Requests and Praises

Today's Date:

My personal request:

Confidential requests from my friends:

I pray that out of His glorious riches He may strengthen you with power through His Spirit in your inner being.   *Ephesians 3:16 NIV*

Notes

UNIT SEVEN

The Refiner's Fire

LESSON ONE
Bloodstained Hands
EZEKIEL 22

LESSON TWO
Sinful Sisters
EZEKIEL 23

LESSON THREE
The Final Judgment
EZEKIEL 24:1-14

LESSON FOUR
Inexpressible Grief
EZEKIEL 24:15-27

LESSON ONE   *Bloodstained Hands*   EZEKIEL 22

Invite the Holy Spirit to lead, direct, teach, and counsel you through the Word of the Lord today.

𐤉𐤄𐤅𐤄

We are coming to the grand finale of the prophecy regarding the fall of Jerusalem and judgment on the nation of Israel. Look at the following outline[1] of the book of Ezekiel to review what the Lord has said thus far and to gain an overview of what He will soon announce through Ezekiel.

1. The Prophet's Call (Chapters 1-3)
   a. Seeing God's glory – 1
   b. Hearing God's Word – 2
   c. Becoming God's Watchman – 3
2. The Fall of Jerusalem (Chapters 4-24)
   a. The judgment predicted -4-7
   b. God's glory departs – 8-11
   c. Godless leaders exposed – 12-17
   d. God's justice defended – 18-21
   e. The end of the city – 22-24
3. The nations judged (Chapters 25-32)
   a. Ammon – 25:1-7
   b. Moab – 25:8-11
   c. Edom – 25:12-24
   d. Philistia – 25:15-17
   e. Tyre – 26:1-28:19
   f. Sidon – 28:20-24
   g. Egypt – 29-32
4. The glorious future of Israel (Chapters 33-48)
   a. The city of Jerusalem restored – 33-34
   b. The land of Israel renewed – 35-36
   c. The nation of Israel resurrected and reunited – 37-39
   d. The temple and the priesthood reestablished – 40-48

Through our studies so far, we have learned that the nation of Israel was rebellious against the ways of the Lord. The kings, prophets, priests and all the people repeatedly disobeyed the Lord with a calloused heart, refusing to listen to the words of warning given by the Lord through His messengers. The Word of the Lord to Ezekiel in Chapter 22 will once again declare the habitual sins of the nation to the Israelites in Babylonian captivity.

Please read the following verses and record those that the Lord holds accountable for the sins of the nation.

Ezekiel 22:1-2

Ezekiel 22:6, 27

Ezekiel 22:25, 28

Ezekiel 22:26

Ezekiel 22:29

Who was held responsible, and who would be judged for the sins of the nation?

There is no date recorded for this particular Word of the Lord to Ezekiel, but the timing of judgment on Israel is indicated. Read Ezekiel 22:1-5 and note the phrases which indicate timing.

The last date given so far was in Ezekiel 20:1, the seventh year, in the fifth month, on the tenth day of the month. In terms that we understand a little better, this was around July or August of 591 BC. History records that Nebuchadnezzar began his attack on Jerusalem in 588 BC. The nation of Israel had no more than three years before the extreme judgment that they deserved would begin, and it may have been closer than that.

What were the specific sins of each of the groups addressed in this chapter? List them below.

The city: Ezekiel 22:3-4

The princes (kings): Ezekiel 22:6-7, 27

The prophets: Ezekiel 22:25,28

The priests: Ezekiel 22:26

The people: Ezekiel 22:29

Take a moment and reflect on the Ten Commandments (Exodus 20:1-17) which gave an overview of the behavior that the Lord desired from His people. How would you describe the sins listed above in light of the Ten Commandments?

The kings had been given a very clear command which was to be a foundation for their ruling of the nation of Israel. According to Deuteronomy 17:18-20, what were they to do and why?

Are the people who are leaders among you reading the Word of God, fearing the Lord, and following His commands? Are you following the right leaders?

What are the consequences that all of the people of Israel brought upon themselves according to the following verses?

Ezekiel 22:4-5

Ezekiel 22:13-16

Ezekiel 22:31

Let's look closely at one more description given in this chapter of the consequences of Israel's sins. Read Ezekiel 22:17-22. Underline, circle, or highlight the words dross, fire, and melt.

Ezekiel 22:17-22: ¹⁷The word of the LORD came to me, saying, ¹⁸ "Son of man, the house of Israel has become dross to Me; they *are* all bronze, tin, iron, and lead, in the midst of a furnace; they have become dross from silver. ¹⁹Therefore thus says the Lord GOD: 'Because you have all become dross, therefore behold, I will gather you into the midst of Jerusalem. ²⁰As *men* gather silver, bronze, iron, lead, and tin into the midst of a furnace, to blow fire on it, to melt *it;* so I will gather *you* in My anger and in My fury, and I will leave *you there* and melt you. ²¹Yes, I will gather you and blow on you with the fire of My wrath, and you shall be melted in its midst. ²²As silver is melted in the midst of a furnace, so shall you be melted in its midst; then you shall know that I, the LORD, have poured out My fury on you.'"

Do you remember the many times that the Lord has prophesied through Ezekiel that the land will be burned with fire? In this very chapter, the Lord says: "I, the LORD, have spoken,, and will do it." (Ezekiel 22:14 You looked at 2 Kings in previous studies: He (Nebuchadnezzar) burned the house of the Lord and the king's house; all the houses of Jerusalem, that is, all the houses of the great, he burned with fire."

Look up the definition for the following word in a lexicon and a Bible dictionary:

Dross: Strong's #5509

Hebrew word:

Hebrew definition:

The process of refining silver described in the verses above is still used today. Silver is usually found combined with other materials and must be "smelted" to be separated. Here is an explanation of smelting from the Encyclopedia Britannica: "Separation of gold or silver from impurities by melting the impure metal in a cupel (a flat, porous dish made of a refractory, or high temperature-resistant material) and then directing a blast of hot air on it in a special furnace. The impurities, including lead, copper, tin, and other unwanted metals, are oxidized and partly vaporized."[2]

Read Ezekiel 22:17-22 once again and summarize the Lord's purpose based on what you have just learned.

God has to hurt a man deeply before he can use him greatly.[3]

A. W. Tozer

Are you experiencing a time of refining in your life right now? What are some of the impurities that the Lord is melting away?

There is one more verse that we need to spend some time looking at before leaving this chapter. Please read Ezekiel 22:30. What was the Lord looking for and why?

Look up the following word from the phrase: "make a wall."

Make: Strong's #1443

Hebrew word:

Hebrew definition:

The Ten Commandments and instructions from the law of the Lord had given boundaries and a hedge of protection to the Israelites, but they had broken down this wall.

Look up the following word from the phrase: "stand in the gap."

Gap: Strong's #6556

Hebrew word:

Hebrew definition:

"To stand in the gap" is a call to intercede on behalf of the people. This was demonstrated by Moses according to Psalm 106:23: "Therefore He said that He would destroy them, had not Moses His chosen one stood before Him in the breach, to turn away His wrath, lest He destroy them."

Stand in the gap. Be a part of building up the wall. Pray for a particular person or group of people that need to turn back to the Lord.

| LESSON TWO | *Sinful Sisters* | EZEKIEL 23 |

"Give me one pure and holy passion…give me one magnificent obsession….give me one glorious ambition for my life….to know and follow hard after You." [4] Make this your prayer today.

יהוה

The words to the song and prayer above are in direct contrast to the words and actions of the nation of Israel described in Ezekiel 23. The Lord desires and deserves our complete devotion but we wander away so often. The people of Israel, the kings, priests, and so-called prophets, pursued their passion to be like other nations rather than to be set apart as a chosen people. Once again the Word of the Lord came to Ezekiel in a graphic manner to condemn the lifestyles of the Israelites.

Please read Ezekiel 23:1-4. In this parable, who are the characters, and what do they represent?

Look up the meaning of the following words and check a Bible dictionary for further explanation of these words.

Oholah: Strong's #170
Hebrew word:
Hebrew definition:

Oholibah: Strong's #172
Hebrew word:
Hebrew definition:

Turn to 1 Kings 11:1-10 and note what you learn about the beginning of idolatry in Jerusalem, the capital city of the Southern Kingdom of Judah.

Samaria became the capital city of the Northern Kingdom of Israel. Turn to 1 Kings 12:28-31 and note what King Jeroboam did that began idolatrous practices in the Northern Kingdom.

Please read Ezekiel 23:5-27. Notice the repeated mention of "harlot" and "Egypt."

Where did the Israelite nation first become involved in idolatry and immorality?

Please read Ezekiel 23:28-35. What is the purpose of the judgment of the Lord according to these verses?

The sins of the cities of Samaria and Jerusalem were pointed out through the vivid parable of the two sisters. And then the Lord explained His own parable in straightforward terms so that the sin and its penalty could be clearly understood.

Please read Ezekiel 23:36-41 and list the sins of Samaria and Jerusalem declared by Ezekiel.

Read Ezekiel 23:42-49 and describe the consequences of the harlotry of these cities.

You may have noticed in an earlier passage the phrase "they shall remove your nose and your ears." This was an ancient punishment for adultery. Another punishment for adultery according to the law of the Lord is also prophesied in this passage.

According to verses 46 and 47, what would happen?

Once again, the Lord was keeping the word of His law. Look at the following references and describe the sin and punishment required.

Leviticus 20:2-3

Deuteronomy 17:2-5

Deuteronomy 22:20-21

In His justice, the Lord never forgets His ultimate goal. He always reminds His people that He has a plan. According to Ezekiel 23:48-49, what will be the outcome of His judgment?

We observed in previous lessons that even the people of the New Testament churches were exhorted to have nothing to do with idolatry. Let's look at a particular passage in which Paul told the people not to repeat the history of the Israelites.

Read 1 Corinthians 10:6-11. What are the admonitions to believers in this passage?

What is the root of the sin of idolatry according to verse 6 in the same passage? How would you explain this in your own words?

Whatever a man seeks, honors, or exalts more than God, is idolatry. [5]

William Bernard Ullanthorne (1806–1889)

Is there any change in lifestyle that you need to make as a result of the lesson learned today?

LESSON THREE　　　　*The Final Judgment*　　　　EZEKIEL 24:1-14

Please pray that you will be open to the counsel and conviction of the Holy Spirit today.

𐤉𐤄𐤅𐤄

The climax of the prophecy of the Lord arrives in the Scriptures that we will study today and tomorrow. The dates given are crucial. The description of the city of Jerusalem is the final declaration of the reason for judgment. After Ezekiel 24, we will see prophecies regarding judgment on other nations, and then we will see prophecies regarding the restoration of the land of Israel and prophecies regarding worship during the reign of the Lord Jesus Christ in the Millennial Kingdom.

Please read Ezekiel 24:1-2. There are seven words or phrases used in these two verses to indicate timing. Fill in the blanks below with these.

(1)_____, in the (2)_____ _____, in the (3)_____ _____, on the (4)_____ _____ of the month, the word of the LORD came to me, saying, "son of man, write down the name of the (5)_____, (6)_____ _____ _____ - the king of Babylon started his siege against Jerusalem (7)_____ _____ _____.

In Day One, we observed that the Lord said Israel "had made her days to draw near" and she had "come to the end of her days." (Ezekiel 22:4) The prophecy in Chapter 22 indicated that even though false prophets had decreed false hope, the days of judgment were soon to come.

Look at the following timeline and fill in the blanks. The years given are the number of years that Israel had been in captivity.

Vision of the Glory of the Lord	Vision of Idolatry in the Temple in Jerusalem	Declarations of Sins of Israel	Announcement of Beginning of Siege against Jerusalem	Message of Destruction of Jerusalem received
Ezekiel 1:1	**Ezekiel 8:1**	**Ezekiel 20:1**	**Ezekiel 24:1**	**Ezekiel 33:21**
5th year,	6th year,	7th year,	____ year,	12th year,
5th day,	5th day,	10th day,	____ day,	5th day,
4th month	6th month	5th month	____ month	10th month
593 BC	592 BC	591 BC	588 BC	585 BC

148

Highlight the dates given in the following verse:

2 Kings 25:1 Now it came to pass in the ninth year of his reign, in the tenth month, on the tenth day of the month, that Nebuchadnezzar king of Babylon and all his army came against Jerusalem and encamped against it; and they built a siege wall against it all around.

Could this be any more clear? The dates given in Ezekiel and in 2 Kings are identical. Even though the books were written by different human authors, the true author of Scripture, the Lord, has kept His facts and dates straight and consistent. May this cause you to grow in your faith and trust of the Word of the Lord.

I love what J. Vernon McGee says about this passage:

There was no television in that day to let Ezekiel know what was happening. There was no satellite to convey this message from Jerusalem to Babylon. The only way he could get this message was by God revealing it to him.[6]

The Lord continued to reveal incredible truths to Ezekiel. In Ezekiel 24:3-13, the Word of the Lord paints a word-picture of the city, and it isn't a pretty one. Please read this passage.

The parable is stated in verses 3, 4, and 5 and the explanation of it is given in verses 6-13. What is the parable or symbol given of Jerusalem?

Record what you learn from the explanation of this poetic parable, using commentaries for additional information.

Ezekiel 24:6 – what is in the pot?

Ezekiel 24:10 – what will happen to the cuts of meat in the pot?

Ezekiel 24:11 – what will happen to the pot itself?

The Lord points His finger at the guilty city, the responsible people, and declares that their wickedness was no accident, but that in their filthiness was lewdness (Ezekiel 24:13).

Look up the definitions for the following words:

Filthiness: Strong's #2932

Hebrew word:

Hebrew definition:

Lewdness: Strong's #2154

Hebrew word:

Hebrew definition:

In today's court systems, the penalty for crimes is more severe when evidence exists for premeditation of the crime. The people of Israel embraced, planned, and defended their idolatry and rebellion against the Lord. There was no other way for the Israelites to be purged, or cleansed from their sins, but by the fire of the wrath of the Lord.

The next verse that you will read is the final Word of the Lord regarding the coming of His judgment. What does He say in Ezekiel 24:14?

What do you learn about the Lord from this verse?

Our Lord is the Most Holy God. The One and Only. He alone is righteous and pure. All of His actions are perfect. Every person ever created deserves the same judgment that the Israelites received because everyone at some point in his or her life has ignored or rebelled against the Lord.

But the Israelites were given hope. They were given the promise of a new heart and a new spirit. They were given the promise of returning to the Lord and knowing Him. And the same is true for you. The Lord sent His Son Jesus to endure the death that we all deserved. At the cross, we each have the opportunity to be cleansed from all our filthiness, even that which was carried out intentionally. At the cross, we each have the opportunity to be spared from the judgment of the Lord.

Turn to Hebrews 9:27-28 and record the truth you learn from this Scripture.

If you have trusted in Christ as your Savior, will you be judged and punished for your sins?

Please read Romans 5:8-9 and record what Christ did for us through His blood, and what He saved us from.

Please read Romans 5:18-19 and record what you learn regarding judgment and justification.

Please look up the definition of the following word in its original language. (Notice that it's Greek this time!)

Justified: Strong's #1344

Greek word:

Greek definition:

Do you remember what the Lord told Ezekiel (in Chapter 14) about the Israelite heroes? "Even if these three men, Noah, Daniel, and Job, were in the land, they would deliver only themselves by their righteousness." Those three great men of faith and righteousness couldn't have saved Israel from the judgment they deserved. But there was one Man sent by God the Father and by His obedience many have been saved and made righteous.

Because of the cross, if you believe that you deserve the judgment of the Lord due to your sins, and if you believe that Jesus Christ received that judgment in your place, then you are forgiven...spared...saved...delivered from judgment. Because of the cross, mercy has been poured out instead of wrath. This gives you a reason to celebrate!

What is your response to the Lord regarding your justification?

LESSON FOUR   *Inexpressible Grief*   EZEKIEL 24:15-27

Please quiet yourself before the Lord asking Him to give you acceptance of the trials that He allows to come in your life.

יהוה

Today's lesson is full of emotion – held in check. The pain is overwhelming but must remain unexpressed. On this day in Ezekiel's life, the Lord's judgment on the nation of Israel has begun. All that He has declared will happen is happening. Nebuchadnezzar has begun his attack against the city of Jerusalem.

The people are now trapped inside the city walls. Fear is spreading and famine is soon to follow. Then the sword and the fire. And death.

All that the Lord has spoken through Ezekiel will come to pass. But the prophet's service is not over. There is much, much more that the Lord will communicate through him.

Read Ezekiel 24:15-18. What did the Lord do in Ezekiel's life?

Look up the definition for the following word:

Desire: Strong's #4261

Hebrew word:

Hebrew definition:

Please list the commands that the Lord gives Ezekiel in this situation.

1.
2.
3.
4.
5.
6.
7.
8.

❖❖❖❖❖❖❖❖❖❖❖❖❖❖❖❖❖❖❖❖❖❖❖❖❖❖❖❖❖❖❖❖

On occasions of mourning it was customary to uncover the head and strew ashes upon it, to go barefoot, and to cover the beard, that is to say, the lower part of the face as far as the nose. [7]

❖❖❖❖❖❖❖❖❖❖❖❖❖❖❖❖❖❖❖❖❖❖❖❖❖❖❖❖❖❖❖❖

The Lord was requiring Ezekiel to forego all the cultural customs of mourning, and commanding him not to express his mourning over his wife in any way.

Can you imagine being told not to grieve over the death of your beloved soul-mate? What are your thoughts about this requirement placed on Ezekiel? How do you think he felt?

In spite of how he may have felt, what did he do according to Ezekiel 24:18?

I am grieving now for Ezekiel and the death of his dear wife. In heaven, all tears will be wiped away, so I don't expect to grieve with him then, but I hope to show my incredible respect to him for his complete obedience to the Lord at what was probably the most difficult sacrifice anyone has ever had to make. Have you heard the stories of missionaries whose sons and daughters or husbands and wives have died tragically on the mission field? They have been required to make extreme sacrifices, but they have been allowed to express their grief as those around them watched.

Is the Lord requiring the sacrifice, the death of something very dear to your heart? Consider Ezekiel, the obedient servant of the Lord. What is the Lord commanding you to do?

The Lord's ways are higher than our ways. He has His reasons for what He brings about in our lives. The people who watched Ezekiel break with the custom of mourning did exactly what the Lord knew they would do.

Read Ezekiel 24:19-24.

What did the people do when they saw Ezekiel's strange behavior?

What parallel to the death of Ezekiel's wife is given in verse 21?

The delight of the soul of the Israelites was the city of God, Jerusalem. Psalm 48 is a song of praise expressing the delight of the people in the city and in their God.

Great is the Lord, and greatly to be praised in the city of our God, in His holy mountain. Beautiful in elevation, the joy of the whole earth, is Mount Zion on the sides of the north, the city of the great King. Psalm 48:1-2^{NKJ}

Keep this perspective in mind as you consider what the people are commanded to do.

Look at your list of commands given to Ezekiel, and beside them, record the parallel commands given to the house of Israel in Ezekiel:24:22-23.

Look up the meaning of the following word:
Mourn: Strong's #5594
Hebrew word:
Hebrew definition:

Pine away: Strong's #4743
Hebrew word:
Hebrew definition:

What would be the reason for the grief of the exiles according to Leviticus 26:39?

The ultimate grief and mourning of the nation of Israel is still in the future. What will bring about their deepest sorrow according to Zechariah 12:10-14?

"Thus Ezekiel is a sign to you; according to all that he has done you shall do; and when this comes, you shall know that I am the Lord God." (Ezekiel 24:24) The reason for it all. That they may know the Lord.

Do you recognize that this is the reason for all that happens in your life? What is the Lord doing in your life to cause you to know Him more intimately?

As we come to the close of this portion of the book of Ezekiel, the Lord gives important information to Ezekiel. Read Ezekiel 24:25-27 and summarize what you learn.

Turn back to Ezekiel 3:26-27 and record what the Lord told Ezekiel at his commissioning as a prophet.

Jump ahead to Ezekiel 33:21-22 and record what happens in these verses.

From the 5ᵗʰ year of captivity until the 12ᵗʰ year of captivity, Ezekiel had been "mute," by the Lord's definition: he was unable to speak anything except what the Lord gave him to say. The messages that Ezekiel had been given to preach and demonstrate to the exiles were all messages of judgment.

And now that judgment has come upon Jerusalem. The destruction which had been prophesied was taking place. Ezekiel will soon be able to speak freely, but not yet. In the years that will pass as Jerusalem is completely destroyed, Ezekiel will open his mouth with more messages from the Lord that announce the destruction of all the nations that have come against Israel. The reason for it all will be declared over and over again.

What is the last statement of the Lord in Ezekiel 24:27?

Reviewing the Revelations

Unit Seven

The Refiner's Fire

Ezekiel 22—24

What were the most meaningful Scriptures or truths from this unit's lessons?

How do these truths impact your daily life?

Is there anything that you have questions about?

Prayer Requests and Praises

Today's Date:

My personal request:

Confidential requests from my friends:

I call to God, and the Lord saves me. Evening, morning and noon I cry out in distress, and He hears my voice.   *Psalm 55:16-17 NIV*

Notes

UNIT EIGHT

Foreign Policies

LESSON ONE
Nasty Neighbors
EZEKIEL 25 and 26

LESSON TWO
A Sinking Ship
EZEKIEL 27 and 28

LESSON THREE
Homeland Security
EZEKIEL 28:25 – 30:26

LESSON FOUR
Pride and Punishment
EZEKIEL 31 and 32

LESSON ONE   *Nasty Neighbors*   EZEKIEL 25 AND 26

Be still and know that He is God. Pray that you will understand His sovereignty more and more as you study today.

יהוה

There are passages in Isaiah, Jeremiah, and Ezekiel that are rich with declarations of love and promises of hope. Even in the minor prophets you will find precious truths that will refresh you. But you will also discover many long difficult passages regarding judgment and the destruction of nations which are not to be found on our modern maps. These passages are the ones in which it is hard to find an encouraging word or devotional thought. These are the type of passages that we will be digging into in this unit.

But I hope through our study today and this week that you will persevere through a few more chapters of prophecy regarding the wrath of the Lord, and that through this study you will see the character of the Lord. It is in knowing Who the Lord is in His entirety that we have rest and security and understanding.

We will move quickly through Ezekiel 25 observing the nations that the Lord moves Ezekiel to speak against and the reasons for judgment against them. Read the following chapter and circle, highlight, or underline the following using three different colors:

1. each nation mentioned
2. each occurrence of the word "because" and the reason following it
3. each repetition of the phrase "then you shall know that I am the Lord"

Ezekiel 25 ¹The word of the LORD came to me, saying, ² "Son of man, set your face against the Ammonites, and prophesy against them. ³Say to the Ammonites, 'Hear the word of the Lord GOD! Thus says the Lord GOD: "Because you said, 'Aha!' against My sanctuary when it was profaned, and against the land of Israel when it was desolate, and against the house of Judah when they went into captivity, ⁴indeed, therefore, I will deliver you as a possession to the men of the East, and they shall set their encampments among you and make their dwellings among you; they shall eat your fruit, and they shall drink your milk. ⁵And I will make Rabbah a stable for camels and Ammon a resting place for flocks. Then you shall know that I *am* the LORD."

⁶ 'For thus says the Lord GOD: "Because you clapped *your* hands, stamped your feet, and rejoiced in heart with all your disdain for the land of Israel, ⁷indeed, therefore, I will stretch out My hand against you, and give you as plunder to the nations; I will cut you off from the peoples, and I will cause you to perish from the countries; I will destroy you, and you shall know that I am the LORD."

⁸ 'Thus says the Lord GOD: "Because Moab and Seir say, 'Look! The house of Judah *is* like all the nations,' ⁹therefore, behold, I will clear the territory of Moab of cities, of the cities on its frontier, the glory of the country, Beth Jeshimoth, Baal Meon, and Kirjathaim. ¹⁰To the men of the East I will give it as a possession, together with the Ammonites, that the Ammonites may not be remembered among the nations. ¹¹And I will execute judgments upon Moab, and they shall know that I am the LORD."

¹² 'Thus says the Lord GOD: "Because of what Edom did against the house of Judah by taking vengeance, and has greatly offended by avenging itself on them," ¹³therefore thus says the Lord GOD: "I will also stretch out My hand against Edom, cut off man and beast from it, and make it desolate from Teman; Dedan shall fall by the sword. ¹⁴I will lay My vengeance on Edom by the hand of My people Israel, that they may do in Edom according to My anger and according to My fury; and they shall know My vengeance," says the Lord GOD.

¹⁵ 'Thus says the Lord GOD: "Because the Philistines dealt vengefully and took vengeance with a spiteful heart, to destroy because of the old hatred," ¹⁶therefore thus says the Lord GOD: "I will stretch out My hand against the Philistines, and I will cut off the Cherethites and destroy the remnant of the seacoast. ¹⁷I will execute great vengeance on them with furious rebukes; and they shall know that I am the LORD, when I lay My vengeance upon them."'"

What would you say is the general reason that the Lord will judge these nations?

What principle does the Lord establish for Himself according to the following verses?

Genesis 12:3

Exodus 23:22

Summarize according to Ezekiel 25 what will happen to each of the nations below:

Ammon (meaning tribal, that is, inbred; Ammon, a son of Lot, also his posterity and their country: - Ammon, Ammonites.) [1]

Moab (meaning from her (the mother's) father; Moab, an incestuous son of Lot; also his territory and descendants: - Moab)[2]

Edom (meaning red; Edom, the elder twin-brother of Jacob; hence the region (Idumaea) occupied by him: - Edom, Edomites, Idumaea.)[3]

Philistia (meaning rolling, that is, migratory; Pelesheth, a region of Syria: - Palestina, Palestine, Philistia, Philistines.)[4]

Where are they now? Read their histories from commentaries below.

Ammon: Ancient historical records mention Ammon's subjugation by Nebuchadnezzar five years after the fall of Jerusalem. Arab invaders came to dominate the territory, and Persian control began about 530 BC.[6] Rabbath-moab and Heshbon (modern *Rabba* and *Hesbân*) are miserable villages, and the country is subject to the raids of the Bedouin tribes of the neighboring desert, which discourages agriculture. But the land is still good pasture ground for cattle and sheep, as in ancient times[7]

Moab: Noldeke says that the extinction of the Moabites was about A.D. 200, at the time when the Yemen tribes Galib and Gassara entered the eastern districts of the Jordan. Since AD536, the last trace of the name, Moab, which lingered in the town of *Kir-moab,* has given place to *Kerak,* its modern name. Over the whole region are scattered many ruins of ancient cities; and while the country is almost bare of larger vegetation, it is still a rich pasture-ground, with occasional fields of grain. The land thus gives evidence of its former wealth and power.[7]

Edom: They gave what help they could to Nebuchadnezzar, and exulted in the destruction of Jerusalem, stirring the bitterest indignation in the hearts of the Jews. The Edomites pressed into the now empty lands in the South of Judah. In 300 BC Mt. Seir with its capital Petra fell into the hands of the Nabateans.[8]

Philistia Destruction came upon them in the general ruin of the inhabitants of Canaan, which commenced with the destruction of Jerusalem by Nebuchadnezzar.[9] This powerful tribe made frequent incursions against the Hebrews. There was almost perpetual war between them. They sometimes held the tribes, especially the southern tribes, in degrading servitude; at other times they were defeated with great slaughter. These hostilities did not cease till the time of Hezekiah, when they were entirely subdued. They still, however, occupied their territory, and always showed their old hatred to Israel. They were finally conquered by the Romans.[10]

In spite of the fact that the Israelites didn't obey the Lord, He still was on their side. He followed through on His promise to curse those who curse them, to protect them, to be their adversary, to take vengeance on anyone who stood against their nation. The Lord first judged His own people for their rebellion against Him, then He judged the pagan, Gentile nations for their rejection of His people and His deity.

"If the righteous will be recompensed on the earth, how much more the wicked and the sinner?"   Proverbs 11:31

Ezekiel 25 was basically a warm-up exercise for us before we move into Chapter 26. In the next three chapters, the Lord communicates much to the nation of Tyre. Today we will cover Ezekiel 26 and in tomorrow's lesson we will cover Ezekiel 27 and 28.

Read Ezekiel 26:1-6. What is the reason for the Lord's judgment, and what will be the ultimate result?

Read Ezekiel 26:7-14. How will the Lord's judgment be carried out?

What do you learn about the culture of Tyre from verses 12 and 13?

Read Ezekiel 26:15-18. What kind of reaction will observers have regarding the destruction of Tyre?

Read Ezekiel 26:19-21. What were the consequences to the nation of Tyre as a result of its pride and evil attitude toward Israel?

Where is Tyre now? "Though you are sought for, you will never be found again." (Ezekiel 26:21) Modern day Lebanon boasts that Tyre is its fourth largest city. In 1979 UNESCO declared Tyre a World Heritage Site. You can take a tour to see the archeological finds of ancient Tyre, and eat at a local seafood restaurant. Do these facts contradict Ezekiel's prophecy?

Consider the following timeline of the history of the city:

585: A 13-year long siege starts under the command of the Babylonian king Nebuchadnezzar 2.

332: After a seven month siege and as the last of the Phoenician cities, Tyre is conquered by the troops of the Macedonian king Alexander the Great. During this time, they build a causeway from the mainland to the island of Tyre, thereby taking away the city's natural defence. Ten thousand of the inhabitants were killed, and 30,000 more sold into slavery.

Alexander literally fulfilled the words **break down your walls** (see v. 5) when his army built a causeway half a mile long between the shore and the city on its island. He tore down defensive walls to build the causeway.[11]

200: Becomes part of the Hellenistic Seleucid kingdom.

68: Passes over to Roman control.

2nd century CE: Tyre is reported to have a sizable Christian community.

638: Conquered by Arab Muslims.

1124: Conquered by Christian Crusaders.

1291: Conquered, and then destroyed by Muslim Mamluks. Tyre would never recover from this blow.

1516: Tyre comes, together with the rest of Lebanon, under Ottoman control.[12]

Tyre was originally built on an island right off the coast, providing for natural defence. Many functions were established on the mainland as well, but all important institutions remained on the island. But from 332BC on, a causeway connected the island to the mainland, making it a peninsula. Tyre was for centuries the strongest and most important Phoenician city, exercising control over the others from 10th century BCE and onwards. The city was famous for its silk products, and its purple dye extracted from the Murex snail. The old harbour area has been excavated, but most of the Phoenician city lies under the modern city.[13]

Today's study has been quite the history, sociology and geography lesson. Are you wondering what difference it makes in your life? Please remember that all that we are studying, and all that has happened down through the ages, in every geographical location is not just "history," but is "His-story." The earth is the Lord's and the fullness thereof.

At the beginning of this lesson, I encouraged you to "be still and know that He is God." Do you know what happens when you do this? Please close today by looking at the rest of the verse from which I am quoting: Psalm 46:10. Keep this verse in mind as we continue our study this week.

LESSON TWO   *A Sinking Ship*   EZEKIEL 27 AND 28

Humble thyself in the sight of the Lord. Bow down before Him and acknowledge Him as your Lord and your God.

יהוה

The city of Tyre was judged because of its pride, and its rulers were judged for their pride as well. If you are not familiar with these chapters, I think you will find some interesting surprises. We will read Ezekiel 27 with our highlighters in hand to take in the various details that are mentioned, then we will spend the majority of this lesson looking at Ezekiel 28.

Ezekiel 27 has portions that would have been recognized in the Hebrew language as poetry, a song, or a funeral dirge. As the Lord has done so often through Ezekiel, He once again uses a metaphor to describe Tyre, likening it to a ship, because of the location of the city on an island as well as because of their extensive trading with other countries.

Please read the following version of Ezekiel 27 and using different colors, circle, highlight or underline the following:

1. each country or nation mentioned
2. each reference to a ship or part of a ship

   GOD's Message came to me: "You, son of man, raise a funeral song over Tyre.

"Tell Tyre, gateway to the sea, merchant to the world, trader among the far-off islands, 'This is what GOD, the Master, says: " 'You boast, Tyre: "I'm the perfect ship--stately, handsome." You ruled the high seas from a real beauty, crafted to perfection. Your planking came from Mount Hermon junipers. A Lebanon cedar supplied your mast. They made your oars from sturdy Bashan oaks. Cypress from Cyprus inlaid with ivory was used for the decks. Your sail and flag were of colorful embroidered linen from Egypt. Your purple deck awnings also came from Cyprus. Men of Sidon and Arvad pulled the oars. Your seasoned seamen, O Tyre, were the crew. Ship's carpenters were old salts from Byblos. All the ships of the sea and their sailors clustered around you to barter for your goods.

"'Your army was composed of soldiers from Paras, Lud, and Put, elite troops in uniformed splendor. They put you on the map! Your city police were imported from Arvad, Helech, and Gammad. They hung their shields from the city walls, a final, perfect touch to your beauty.

"'Tarshish carried on business with you because of your great wealth. They worked for you, trading in silver, iron, tin, and lead for your products. Greece, Tubal, and Meshech did business with you, trading slaves and bronze for your products. Beth-togarmah traded work horses, war horses, and mules for your products. The people of Rhodes did business with you. Many far-off islands traded with you in ivory and ebony.

"'Edom did business with you because of all your goods. They traded for your products with agate, purple textiles, embroidered cloth, fine linen, coral, and rubies. Judah and Israel did business with you. They traded for your products with premium wheat, millet, honey, oil, and balm. Damascus, attracted by your vast array of products and well-stocked warehouses, carried on business with you, trading in wine from Helbon and wool from Zahar.

"'Danites and Greeks from Uzal traded with you, using wrought iron, cinnamon, and spices. Dedan traded with you for saddle blankets. Arabia and all the Bedouin sheiks of Kedar traded lambs, rams, and goats with you. Traders from Sheba and Raamah in South Arabia carried on business with you in premium spices, precious stones, and gold. Haran, Canneh, and Eden from the east in Assyria and Media traded with you, bringing elegant clothes, dyed textiles, and elaborate carpets to your bazaars.

"'The great Tarshish ships were your freighters, importing and exporting. Oh, it was big business for you, trafficking the seaways! Your sailors row mightily, taking you into the high seas. Then a storm out of the east shatters your ship in the ocean deep. Everything sinks--your rich goods and products, sailors and crew, ship's carpenters and soldiers, Sink to the bottom of the sea. Total shipwreck. The cries of your sailors reverberate on shore. Sailors everywhere abandon ship. Veteran seamen swim for dry land. They cry out in grief, a choir of bitter lament over you. They smear their faces with ashes, shave their heads, Wear rough burlap, wildly keening their loss. They raise their funeral song: "Who on the high seas is like Tyre!"

"'As you crisscrossed the seas with your products, you satisfied many peoples. Your worldwide trade made earth's kings rich. And now you're battered to bits by the waves, sunk to the bottom of the sea, And everything you've bought and sold has sunk to the bottom with you. Everyone on shore looks on in terror. The hair of kings stands on end, their faces drawn and haggard! The buyers and sellers of the world throw up their hands: This horror can't happen! Oh, this has happened!'"

Using the translation of the Bible that you normally read, answer the following questions according to the verses given:

Ezekiel 26:2 What did Tyre say against Jerusalem?

Ezekiel 27:25 How is Tyre described?

Ezekiel 27:26 What happened to Tyre?

"Then a storm out of the east shatters your ship in the ocean deep." This is a paraphrase of Ezekiel 27:26 and a prophecy of what was to happen to Tyre. Not only did the Lord allow Nebuchadnezzar to carry out His judgment on Israel, but He also allowed Him to be a part of His judgment on Tyre.

The lamentation ends and another proclamation begins. The Lord will state through Ezekiel the judgment to come upon the ruler of Tyre.

Read Ezekiel 28:1-10 and look for *who* this proclamation is spoken against, *why* it is spoken (watch for the word "because") and *what* it is (watch for the word "therefore").

Who:

Why:

What:

Did you notice that in Ezekiel 28:8, the Lord summarizes the destruction of Tyre that He described in Chapters 26 and 27? Look at verse 8 and compare it to the following verses. This is just for you to see the intricacy of the Word of God.

Ezekiel 26:19,20: "...when I bring the deep upon you, and great waters cover you, ²⁰then I will bring you down with those who descend into the Pit..."

Ezekiel 27:27: "...All your men of war who *are* in you, and the entire company which *is* in your midst, will fall into the midst of the seas on the day of your ruin."

The Word of the Lord is completely clear regarding the future of Tyre and its prince. And the Word of the Lord is completely clear regarding the reason for the judgment against this man who didn't think of himself as a man.

According to Ezekiel 28:9-10, how did the Lord plan to give the prince understanding of his humanity?

Arrogant rulers are held accountable before the Lord. The Pharoahs of Egypt saw themselves as gods, and we are now fascinated with their tombs. One in particular experienced the power and wonder of the One True God when he was plagued repeatedly! (Exodus 5:2) Nebuchadnezzar himself, the agent of the Lord for judgment on Israel and Tyre, was brought to his knees for his pride.(Daniel 4) He had to spend seven years grazing fields as if he were a wild animal.

And just read what Herod did and how the Lord judged him:

Acts 12 ²¹So on a set day Herod, arrayed in royal apparel, sat on his throne and gave an oration to them. ²²And the people kept shouting, "The voice of a god and not of a man!" ²³Then immediately an angel of the Lord struck him, because he did not give glory to God. And he was eaten by worms and died.

The application to our lives is easy to grasp. All we have to remember is: "it's not about me." Are you a prideful person? Have you placed yourself on the throne of your life? Are you taking credit for health, home and happiness?

*We have just looked at the proclamation against the **prince** of Tyre in Ezekiel 28:1-10. The next section in Chapter 28 is a "lamentation" addressed to the **King** of Tyre, a figure who may be different from the prince referred to in Ezekiel 28:1. There are descriptions given of this king which seem to indicate that he was more than a human ruler, and this passage could possibly be a description of Satan.*

Please read Ezekiel 28:11-19.

According to Ezekiel 28:12-14, what words or phrases describe the greatness of this king?

According to Ezekiel 28:15-17, what were the sins of this king?

According to Ezekiel 28:18-19, what was the Lord's response to the pride of this king?

*Once again, pride in self and pride in the accomplishments of self are exposed and judged. The ultimate sin in this king was his attitude that he had become like God. This was the temptation that Satan laid before Eve in the Garden. "Then the serpent said to the woman, 'You will not surely die. For God knows that in the day that you eat of it your eyes will be opened, and **you will be like** God, knowing good and evil.'" Genesis 3:4-5.*

You have probably had enough teaching in church that you would never say that you could be like God. But each of us is tempted regularly to behave as if we were God. When we want to do things our way. When we want to understand unexplainable mysteries and doubt the truths of Scripture if we can't get our minds around them. When we want to be in control of our own lives and the lives of those around us. When we think that we deserve praise, reward and success.

The Lord knows Who He is. And He knows who you are. In Christ, you are His special treasure and are being conformed to the very image of Christ. You already have an incredible identity as a child of God. Let God be God! You can't handle His job. He makes the sun rise each day and keeps the planets spinning in their orbits. He never sleeps. He knows the very number of the hairs on your head. Do you?

The next passage that we will look at in Ezekiel 28 is a fitting conclusion to our study today. The result of all the judgments of the Lord is made absolutely clear.

Please read Ezekiel 28:20-24.

The Lord declares that He is bringing judgment against the nation of Sidon in this passage. What will happen as a result?

LESSON THREE — *Homeland Security* — EZEKIEL 29 AND 30

His love endures forever. Pray that today you will grasp the faithfulness of the Lord in your own life.

יהוה

In the midst of seven chapters regarding judgment against the nations surrounding Israel, the Lord inserts an extraordinary promise to His beloved people. There verses stand in radical contrast to the surrounding context. Let's look at what the Lord said, and why He said it here.

Please read Ezekiel 28:25-26.

What is the promise? We need to dissect this verse to see the specifics. I've done a little diagramming of the verse, to make the main sentence structure of subject and verb stand out, with modifying phrases placed below that which they modify. Mark **what the Lord will do** and **what the Israelites will do.** Mark any repeated words. (Remember to look for pronouns.)

[25] 'Thus says the Lord GOD:

"When   I have gathered   the house of Israel

                                from the peoples

                                          among whom they are scattered,

and   am hallowed

                in them

                in the sight of the Gentiles,

then   they will dwell

                in their own land

                        which I gave

                                to My servant Jacob.

[26] And   they will dwell

                safely there,

        build houses,

and   plant vineyards;

yes,   they will dwell

                securely,

                when I execute judgments

                        on all those around them

                              who despise them.

Then   they shall know

                that I am the LORD their God."''

Based on your observations, answer the following questions:

What does the Lord promise that He will do?

What conditions exist in this promise? What has to happen in the nation of Israel before other things happen? What has to happen in the nations surrounding Israel?

What is the reason given by the Lord for Israel to have "their own land"?

What can the nation of Israel begin to anticipate?

Reflect on what we've studied in the previous 28 chapters of Ezekiel. I'd summarize most of it as gloom and doom, wouldn't you? We have noticed the various promises and encouraging words of the Lord, but most of His statements have been regarding the horrible sins of Israel and His judgment on the nation because of them. Over and over again the Lord declared that the people and the land would be judged. The people would be killed by the sword, by famine, by fire. The land would be ravaged. It would be as desolate as the wilderness. The word "land" is repeated 153 times in the book of Ezekiel. The actual territory that the Lord gave to His chosen people, the Israelites, is of extreme importance. It's true today.

Using your imagination, think about how Ezekiel and his audience would have reacted to the words of the Lord in Ezekiel 28:25-26. How did they feel before and after this statement? You may also want to look at Psalm 137.

This moment of hope, this anticipation of peace, this possibility of joy was dropped in the midst of proclamations of judgment on the nations surrounding Israel. It was also placed almost immediately following the lamentation for the King of Tyre. Why? What did these topics have to do with each other?

What do you think?

Did you ever work any puzzles that had to be decoded with a piece of red plastic? The words were written in blue and red ink, and you could only read the answer to the puzzle when you covered the print with the red transparent paper. I wish I could do that right here! I hope you've spent some time just thinking about why the Lord would make this promise in the midst of the judgments that He was offering.

All of Scripture is inspired, even the organization and placement of the concepts. Here's my answer to the previous question: The nation of Israel would know that the Lord is on their side because He was going to bring about judgment on the nations surrounding them, specifically because of their attitudes and actions against Israel. The promise of dwelling securely in their land would have seemed possible because the Lord was promising to destroy the surrounding nations. And the greatest enemy of Israel is the same one who is the greatest enemy of the Lord. If the lamentation for the King of Tyre is a description of Satan, then this promise to Israel could be considered a proclamation of the power and promise of the Lord in contrast to the desires of Satan.

With the promise of being gathered and dwelling in their own land, we get a taste of what is to come in the second half of the book of Ezekiel. There's one more nation that has to be dealt with and then the Lord will direct Ezekiel to prophesy about His plans for Israel. Hang in there as we study the proclamation against Egypt for the rest of today and tomorrow!

The Word of the Lord against Egypt is intricate and detailed. We could spend a week's study on the next four chapters. But I chose to cover all of the judgments on Israel's enemies during this unit of study, so today we will do a quick overview of Ezekiel 29 and 30. In the next lesson, we will conclude with Ezekiel 31 and 32. Ready?

Read Ezekiel 29 and 30. Watch for the phrase: "then they shall know that I am the Lord."

How many times is it repeated in these two chapters?

The Lord used a vivid metaphor to describe the Pharaoh and what He will do to him, and then continued to describe the judgment to come upon Egypt. Summarize what was prophesied to Egypt in Ezekiel 29:3-16.

What interesting news was given to Ezekiel in verses 17 and 18, and how was that important to the statement in verses 19 and 20? The words "yet" (NKJV) or "but" (NASB) and "therefore" are crucial to understanding what is being said.

It's a little difficult to see an immediate application of this Word of the Lord to our lives, isn't it? We can certainly be reminded that the actions of the Lord are to lead us to see Him and know that He is the Lord. There's also a phrase in the midst of this chapter that can direct us to do some evaluation of our lives: "No longer shall it [Egypt] be the confidence of the house of Israel." Israel had a long history of turning to Egypt for help instead of turning to the Lord. When Egypt was judged, its cities were turned into abandoned places, the people were scattered throughout the nations, and Egypt lost its powerful status for all time. It was no longer a nation that could help Israel.

Is there something or someone in your own life that you turn to for help instead of turning to the Lord? Has the Lord removed anything or anyone from your life so that you would have to turn to Him instead? What or who do you put your confidence in? Do you realize that the Lord transforms you by changing the circumstances around you?

"Some trust in chariots and some in horses, but we trust in the name of the Lord our God."   Psalm 20:7 NIV

Do you put your trust, your confidence, your security in anything listed below? What would you do if it were removed from your life?

Health	Friends	Family	Money
Education	Possessions	Pastor	Social activities
Employer or Employment		Talents, skills and abilities	

Ezekiel himself experienced quite a change in his circumstances. He was taken from his home in Jerusalem. He was placed in a foreign land. He had been preparing for the priesthood but was seized by the Lord to be a prophet! In Ezekiel 3:24, the Lord said to him: "Go, shut yourself inside your house." His social activities were limited. And, in Ezekiel 3:26, the Lord said: "I will make your tongue cling to the roof of your mouth, so that you shall be mute..." He lost his voice, except for the times when the Lord wanted to speak through him. I continue to be amazed at Ezekiel's surrender and submission to the Lord's plans for him.

What was Ezekiel told in Ezekiel 29:21 that would impact his day to day life?

"In that day." The judgment against Egypt would be a red-letter day for Israel and for Ezekiel! Israel would see that the Lord is keeping His word, and Ezekiel would be able to speak words!

Ezekiel 30 is a further description of what will happen to Egypt and her neighboring allies. Read through this chapter once more, and remember that the Lord is always watching how nations treat His people Israel.

In opposing God's purposes for Israel, Egypt invited God's judgments on their own nation, for the Lord always keeps His covenant promises.[14]
                                                            Warren Wiersbe

---

LESSON FOUR — *Pride and Punishment* — EZEKIEL 31 AND 32

You have free access to the throne room of the Lord God Almighty through the blood of Jesus Christ, but remember to approach Him with a humble heart. Spend time in His magnificent presence before you begin your study today.

יהוה

One more day of judgment on the nations. You just might be thinking, "I really don't care about what happened to Pharaoh!" But the Lord thought it eternally important to proclaim. Through Ezekiel in 585 B.C. and even now in the 21st century. So please persevere in your study once more, as we look at the figurative descriptions of the nations of Assyria and Egypt.

In Ezekiel 31 you will see that most of the chapter describes the nation of Assyria as a great, strong, beautiful cedar tree. Verse 2 and verse 18 are spoken to the Pharaoh of Egypt.

In Ezekiel 32, you will see poetic descriptions of the Pharaoh as a lion and as a sea monster (possibly a crocodile). In verses 17 through 32 you will see those from the underworld taunting the Pharaoh as he joins them in the grave.

Sounds really encouraging doesn't it? Keep this in mind: you take great comfort and relief in knowing that one day in the future, Satan, that enemy of our souls, will be bound and cast into the lake of fire and brimstone where he will be tormented day and night forever and ever. That's good news to us! The judgment and lamentation against Egypt and its Pharaoh was good news to the Israelite exiles. If the Lord is for us, who can stand against us?

Please read Ezekiel 31 and 32.

What interesting statements stand out to you from Ezekiel 31? Repeated words, comparisons, themes, explanations?

What do you learn from Ezekiel 31:9?

What happened to Assyria and why, according to Ezekiel 31:10-14?

Once again, the pride of the rulers of nations is exposed, condemned, and eternally penalized. I expect that few of you are kings, presidents, and rulers, but you may be a leader in your community, school, or church. Beware of subtle pride.

Please turn to Proverbs 29:23 and write out this verse, personalizing it and making it a prayer.

Ezekiel 31:18 sets the stage for the lamentation in Chapter 32. According to that verse, what was the fate of Pharaoh King of Egypt and all his multitude?

Summarize the following sections of Ezekiel 32:

Verses 1-2

Verses 3-8

Verses 9-10

Verses 11-15

In Ezekiel 32:17-32, the Lord gives His final words against the nation of Egypt and concludes His oracles against the nations. Ezekiel is commanded to "wail," which means to groan or cry aloud, over the multitude of Egypt.

Read this passage, Ezekiel 32:17-32, and mark the nations that are in the grave, as well as the repeated word "uncircumcised." Notice the repetition of the words "slain by the sword," "graves," and "shame."

> The Egyptians were very careful in their practice of circumcision, but their ruler would be lying in sheol with the dead from nations that didn't practice it at all. What humiliation! [15]

You've just attended the wakes of seven nations and their rulers. You've heard the truthful eulogies that stated the power and the pride, the greatness and the greed, the dominance and the disdain, of these nations toward the Lord's people, Israel. For their attitude and actions against His chosen nation, they were condemned.

But the Lord had another purpose in mind in addition to judgment on behalf of Israel. Turn back to the beginning of the proclamations against the foreign nations and highlight the phrase repeated in the verses below. What did the Lord purpose for these nations? (One answer fits all!)

Ezekiel 25:5, 7, 11, 17

Ezekiel 26:6

Ezekiel 28:22-23, 26

Ezekiel 29:6, 9, 16, 21

Ezekiel 30:8, 19, 25-26

Ezekiel 32:15

Do you think that the Lord wants people from every nation, tribe, and tongue to know and love Him? How is He getting His message out today?

Are you involved in spreading the truth of the gospel to the world? If so, how?

We did it! We surveyed the foreign policies of the nations surrounding Israel and saw the judgment they received because of them. Let's end our week's study in prayer for today's nations and their leaders whose foreign policies stand in opposition to Israel, and pray for wisdom for those who support Israel.

Thus says the Lord:

> "I will bless those who bless you, and I will curse him who curses you..."

Genesis 12:3

Reviewing the Revelations

Unit Eight

Foreign Policies

Ezekiel 25—32

What were the most meaningful Scriptures or truths from this unit's lessons?

How do these truths impact your daily life?

Is there anything that you have questions about?

Prayer Requests and Praises

Today's Date:

My personal request:

Confidential requests from my friends:

Always keep on praying for all the saints.

Ephesians 6:18 NIV

Notes

UNIT NINE

A Change for the Better

LESSON ONE
And It Came to Pass
EZEKIEL 33:1-22

LESSON TWO
A Prophet Has Been Among Them
EZEKIEL 33:23-33

LESSON THREE
The Best Is Yet to Come
EZEKIEL 34

LESSON FOUR
To the Mountains
EZEKIEL 35:1 — 36:15

LESSON ONE   *And It Came to Pass*   EZEKIEL 33:1-22

Please prepare yourself for study today by spending time in prayer, expressing your dependence on the Holy Spirit to give you understanding of the Word of God.

יהוה

In my Bible, I've drawn two solid lines between the last verse of Ezekiel 32 and the first verse of Ezekiel 33. This is a visual aid that excites me! We are about to embark on the study of the rest of the book of Ezekiel which will be about the future of Israel. And the future of Israel is glorious! This week, we will not be studying seven chapters as we did last week, but instead only three. Isn't that good news?

The Lord inspired Ezekiel to put his book together in an easy-to-follow, logical format. That doesn't mean that everything is easy to understand, but the flow of thought and divisions of the book make sense. In Ezekiel 33, after seven chapters of judgment prophesied against Israel's neighboring nations, the Lord speaks personally to Ezekiel again. He says some things that He has said before. It seems to me that the Lord thought it was a good time for a review. And it's a perfect time in our study for a review as well. In the coming weeks of study, you will encounter brand-new, mind-boggling Scriptures, so enjoy the look back today!

Read Ezekiel 33. I hope you find that this chapter has a familiar ring to it.

Name a few phrases or concepts from this chapter that Ezekiel had already heard from the Lord.

Now please turn back and read Ezekiel 3:16-27.

Compare Ezekiel 33:1-22 with Ezekiel 3:16-27 and note the similarities or related topics that you observe. Record your findings by stating the verses and brief phrases.

Ezekiel 3:16-27	Ezekiel 33:1-22
V17 – I have made you a watchman	V7 – I have made you a watchman

In Unit One, you did quite a bit of study on Ezekiel's role as a watchman. Turn to page 24 and read your definitions of "watchman" and "warning" as well as the scenarios you listed in answer to the questions on page 25.

We've seen Ezekiel in action through 32 chapters. Was he a good watchman? Why or why not?

The Lord was not only reviewing and reminding Ezekiel of his call to be a watchman, but He was also reviewing His message to the house of Israel. Read Ezekiel 33:12-20 again, then turn to Ezekiel 18 and review this chapter. It will also be helpful to turn back to Week Six, Day One, and review the notes you made.

The Lord makes almost identical statements in these two chapters. Using the cross-references in your Bible or a concordance, or just by close examination of these passages, find the verses that are the same. Write out the verse, and record both references.

What do you learn about the Lord from these statements?

The chapter that we are studying contains not only reviews, but also a watershed moment that Ezekiel had been anticipating. What happened in Ezekiel 33:21-22?

From this time on, in Ezekiel's life, in his book, and in our study, everything changes. What, if anything, have you experienced from the hand of the Lord that changed everything?

The Israelites in exile heard the news that what they never thought would happen had happened. They had not believed that Ezekiel's warnings were true. At this point in their lives they became more distraught and depressed than they ever had been before. And it was at this point in their lives that the Lord began to offer them hope in Him and what He would do for them. It was time for a change of heart.

Spend some time examining your perspective on your own circumstances. Are you like the exiled Israelites in any way? Has the Lord spoken to you through His word? Do you believe Him? Are you discouraged? Is it time for a change of heart?

Hope in Him and your future will be glorious.

LESSON TWO *A Prophet Has Been Among Them*   EZEKIEL 33:23-33

Pray that you will hear and obey the Word of the Lord today and every day.

יהוה

*Yesterday we ended our lesson thinking about moments in our lives that change everything. Tomorrow you will see the Lord's first announcement about how things are going to be different. But the end of Ezekiel 33 gives us a few concluding remarks regarding the attitude of those remaining in the ruins of Israel, and the attitude of those who were in exile with Ezekiel. We can learn a few lessons from them about how **not** to act.*

Let's see what they were saying back in Israel. Read Ezekiel 33:23-29 below.

²³Then the word of the LORD came to me, saying: ²⁴ "Son of man, they who inhabit those ruins in the land of Israel are saying, 'Abraham was only one, and he inherited the land. But we are many; the land has been given to us as a possession.'

²⁵ "Therefore say to them, 'Thus says the Lord GOD: "You eat meat with blood, you lift up your eyes toward your idols, and shed blood. Should you then possess the land? ²⁶You rely on your sword, you commit abominations, and you defile one another's wives. Should you then possess the land?"'

²⁷ "Say thus to them, 'Thus says the Lord GOD: "As I live, surely those who are in the ruins shall fall by the sword, and the one who is in the open field I will give to the beasts to be devoured, and those who are in the strongholds and caves shall die of the pestilence. ²⁸For I will make the land most desolate, her arrogant strength shall cease, and the mountains of Israel shall be so desolate that no one will pass through. ²⁹Then they shall know that I am the LORD, when I have made the land most desolate because of all their abominations which they have committed."'

Who are "they"?

There is another description of "them" in Jeremiah 39:10 and Jeremiah 40:7. What else do you learn about "them"?

According to Ezekiel 33:24, what were "they" saying?

Check your Bible's study notes or a commentary to understand what this meant. Record your findings.

Even though the remaining Israelites thought that they had enough people to rebuild the nation, the Lord pointed out the reasons that they would not be allowed to do so. What were they doing?

What would be the consequences of their sin according to Ezekiel 33:27-28?

Please read through the passage above again, this time highlighting, circling or underlining the word "land."

In what condition did the Lord want the land of Israel to be? And why did He want it to be that way?

Nebuchadnezzar and his armies had come through as agents of divine demolition and had burned, torn down, and destroyed everything in Jerusalem. Anything valuable they carried away as spoils of war. The promised land was no longer a beautiful sight; instead it was not much more than a trash heap. Yet there were still some Israelites scavenging through the ruins. With grit and tenacity, with stubbornness and self-preservation in mind, they seemed to say: "We can do it. We will take back our land."

Does this sound like the right attitude to have, after all that you've heard the Lord say to the people through Ezekiel? Here's a harder question: When the Lord disciplines you and brings you to places of brokenness, how do you respond?

"Then they shall know that I am the Lord." That's the wonderful truth to learn from brokenness. The Israelites in the land weren't the only ones who needed an attitude adjustment. The exiles had finally heard the news that Jerusalem had been destroyed, which should have made them understand that Ezekiel really did have a direct connection with the Lord. Look at how their actions and attitudes are described in the following passage.

Read Ezekiel 33:30-33. What were they doing right? What were they doing wrong?

Some things never change. Hearing and not doing. It really started in the Garden. And it has continued and will continue. But let it not be said of you and me.

Look at the following verses and explain how they relate to what we've been studying and how they warn us as well.

Isaiah 29:13

James 1:22-24

If you are having trouble doing what the Lord asks of you, you don't need to try harder. You just need a change of heart. Ask Him for it.

LESSON THREE *The Best Is Yet to Come* **EZEKIEL 34**

Pray that you will hear the voice of your Shepherd today.

יהוה

Today's message in Ezekiel 34 is about shepherds and sheep. There is a cute little nursery rhyme that is about the same subjects. Do you remember Little Bo Peep?

> *Little Bo Peep has lost her sheep*
> *And can't tell where to find them*
> *Leave them alone,*
> *And they'll come home*
> *Wagging their tails behind them*[1]

185

The shepherds you are about to read about in Ezekiel 34 were the previous political rulers in Israel, and they were as irresponsible as Bo Peep. It was time for a change and the Lord is about to make an announcement about His plans.

This chapter is one of contrast and comparison, and one of past mistakes and future blessings. The best way to take it all in will be to mark it up. This exercise is not just busy work; it is to help you grasp the incredible love of the Lord for His people, the sheep of His pasture. One commentator has stated that "it would be difficult indeed to find a more important chapter in the entire Old Testament than this one,"[2] so please take your time and enjoy God's Word!

Color #1: mark the actions of the "shepherds of Israel" (vs.1-8)

Color #2: mark each mention of "My sheep," "My flock"

Color #3: mark the judgment of the Lord against the irresponsible shepherds (vs.7-10)

Color #4: mark the actions of the Lord rescuing His flock (vs.10-16)

Color #5: mark those who will be judged and what their faults were (vs. 17-22)

Color #6: mark the changes and the blessings that the Lord will bring about (vs.23-31)

> It was common with the eastern nations, and with the Greeks, to call kings shepherds; and one and the same word; in the Greek language, signifies to feed sheep, and to govern people.[3]

Ezekiel 34

¹And the word of the LORD came to me, saying, ²"Son of man, prophesy against the shepherds of Israel, prophesy and say to them, 'Thus says the Lord GOD to the shepherds: "Woe to the shepherds of Israel who feed themselves! Should not the shepherds feed the flocks? ³You eat the fat and clothe yourselves with the wool; you slaughter the fatlings, but you do not feed the flock. ⁴The weak you have not strengthened, nor have you healed those who were sick, nor bound up the broken, nor brought back what was driven away, nor sought what was lost; but with force and cruelty you have ruled them. ⁵So they were scattered because *there was* no shepherd; and they became food for all the beasts of the field when they were scattered. ⁶My sheep wandered through all the mountains, and on every high hill; yes, My flock was scattered over the whole face of the earth, and no one was seeking or searching for them."

⁷"Therefore, you shepherds, hear the word of the LORD: ⁸"As I live," says the Lord GOD, "surely because My flock became a prey, and My flock became food for every beast of the field, because there was no shepherd, nor did My shepherds search for My flock, but the shepherds fed themselves and did not feed My flock"—⁹therefore, O shepherds, hear the word of the LORD! ¹⁰Thus says the Lord GOD: "Behold, I am against the shepherds, and I will require My flock at their hand; I will cause them to cease feeding the sheep, and the shepherds shall feed themselves no more; for I will deliver My flock from their mouths, that they may no longer be food for them."

¹¹ 'For thus says the Lord GOD: "Indeed I Myself will search for My sheep and seek them out. ¹²As a shepherd seeks out his flock on the day he is among his scattered sheep, so will I seek out My sheep and deliver them from all the places where they were scattered on a cloudy and dark day. ¹³And I will bring them out from the peoples and gather them from the countries, and will bring them to their own land; I will feed them on the mountains of Israel, in the valleys and in all the inhabited places of the country. ¹⁴I will feed them in good pasture, and their fold shall be on the high mountains of Israel. There they shall lie down in a good fold and feed in rich pasture on the mountains of Israel. ¹⁵I will feed My flock, and I will make them lie down," says the Lord GOD. ¹⁶I will seek what was lost and bring back what was driven away, bind up the broken and strengthen what was sick; but I will destroy the fat and the strong, and feed them in judgment."

¹⁷"And as for you, O My flock, thus says the Lord GOD: "Behold, I shall judge between sheep and sheep, between rams and goats. ¹⁸Is it too little for you to have eaten up the good pasture, that you must tread down with your feet the residue of your pasture—and to have drunk of the clear waters, that you must foul the residue with your feet? ¹⁹And as for My flock, they eat what you have trampled with your feet, and they drink what you have fouled with your feet."

²⁰"Therefore thus says the Lord GOD to them: "Behold, I Myself will judge between the fat and the lean sheep. ²¹Because you have pushed with side and shoulder, butted all the weak ones with your horns, and scattered them abroad, ²²therefore I will save My flock, and they shall no longer be a prey; and I will judge between sheep and sheep. ²³I will establish one shepherd over them, and he shall feed them—My servant David. He shall feed them

and be their shepherd. ²⁴And I, the LORD, will be their God, and My servant David a prince among them; I, the LORD, have spoken.

²⁵"I will make a covenant of peace with them, and cause wild beasts to cease from the land; and they will dwell safely in the wilderness and sleep in the woods. ²⁶I will make them and the places all around My hill a blessing; and I will cause showers to come down in their season; there shall be showers of blessing. ²⁷Then the trees of the field shall yield their fruit, and the earth shall yield her increase. They shall be safe in their land; and they shall know that I am the LORD, when I have broken the bands of their yoke and delivered them from the hand of those who enslaved them. ²⁸And they shall no longer be a prey for the nations, nor shall beasts of the land devour them; but they shall dwell safely, and no one shall make *them* afraid. ²⁹I will raise up for them a garden of renown, and they shall no longer be consumed with hunger in the land, nor bear the shame of the Gentiles anymore. ³⁰Thus they shall know that I, the LORD their God, am with them, and they, the house of Israel, are My people," says the Lord GOD. ³¹"You are My flock, the flock of My pasture; you are men, and I am your God," says the Lord GOD.'"

There is so much for us to consider in this chapter! There is more than we can possibly cover in one day, and probably more than we could cover in a week. The exercise you have just completed should have given you a good overview of this message of hope for the future spoken by the Lord. Judgment on the previous kings of Israel and their political assistants would be carried out, a new regime would be put in place, and the nation of Israel would be led by the One, True, Good Shepherd. In their own land, Israel would be safe, satisfied and set apart unto the Lord.

Fill in the blanks for the verse below.

Ezekiel 34:6: "My sheep_____through all the _____, and on _____ _____ _____; yes, My flock was _____ over the whole face of the earth, and no one was _____ or _____ for them."

Do you remember the message from the Lord in Ezekiel 6? Glance back at that chapter for a moment, or look back at the notes in your study in Unit Two, pages 39-44.

How did the sheep wander? What happened when they wandered?

Please look up the definition for the following words:

Wandered: Strong's #7686

Hebrew word:

Hebrew definition:

Search: Strong's #1875

Hebrew word:

Hebrew definition:

The nation of Israel, the sheep, needed leaders who would search for them when they wandered away from the Lord. But the leaders themselves wandered from Him by worshipping idols and by turning to other nations for security instead of turning to the Lord.

Ezekiel 34:11 is the turning point of the chapter. The Lord sums up everything with just a few words. What is His key statement?

If you want the job done well, do it yourself, right? This is what the Lord wanted from the beginning, but the people didn't want Him. What did the elders of Israel say in 1 Samuel 8:4-7, and what did the Lord say?

Have you experienced a time when the Lord gave you what you asked for, and you realized that it wasn't what was best for you? The Lord is transforming us to be our very best, and He is preparing the very best things for us. He is also preparing the very best for His chosen people, Israel, as we will see as we continue to study this chapter.

According to Ezekiel 34:12,13, from *where* specifically will the Lord gather His people? There are three phrases that describe this.

Where were they when this message was being spoken to them? (The answer to this question is not in this passage!)

To what place will the Lord bring His flock? (Look closely at Ezekiel 34:13)

What will the Lord do for Israel after He brings them back to their land? This is described clearly in the rest of this chapter. List everything you see.

This chapter is the threshold for the rest of the book; in it, we encounter prophecy that has not yet been fulfilled. There were a few short verses prior to this chapter that hinted at hope for Israel, but now the rest of the book will expound on those promises. The Lord paints a rainbow of hope in the skies that have been dark and cloudy with judgment.

If we journeyed back in time to the day that Ezekiel 34 was spoken to the people, we would arrive at 585 BC. Jerusalem had been destroyed, only a few poor and lowly Israelites were in the land, the kings of Israel had been killed or captured, and the people of Israel were scattered. To the human eye, the nation of Israel was no more. But the Word of the Lord came to Ezekiel! And the Lord promised to deliver His people from their captivity, to make them dwell safely in their own land, to establish One Shepherd among them, and He promised that they would be His people, and He would be with them and be their God. Then they would know that He is the Lord! For Israel, the best is yet to come.

What do you think is the best part of all that the Lord promises to Israel? Why?

We'll continue to study and learn about the Lord's promises to Israel as we move through the rest of Ezekiel. It's hard to leave this chapter... it is overflowing with the goodness and faithfulness of the Lord. The nation of Israel has much to hope for because of who they are. So do we.

> May the eyes of your understanding be enlightened; that you may know what is the hope of His calling, what are the riches of the glory of His inheritance in the saints, and what is the exceeding greatness of His power toward us who believe.
> Ephesians 1:17-19

LESSON FOUR — *To the Mountains* — EZEKIEL 35:1-36:15

Please stop and trust the Lord to open your eyes to His truths every time you study His word.

יהוה

When you begin to read the next passage of Scripture, you might think: "I thought you said that the rest of Ezekiel was about the promises of the Lord for Israel! Here we go with judgment again!" You're right! But the judgment described is one of the evidences that the Lord gives Israel that He is going to prepare a place for them to dwell safely. When their enemies are destroyed, there will be no threat to the nation. Read the next assignment with that in mind.

Before you read the passage, I would like you to see to whom the Lord directs this prophecy. Who is the son of man to prophesy against according to Ezekiel 35:2?

Who is he to prophesy to according to Ezekiel 36:1?

Now please read Ezekiel 35:1 – 36:15.

What are the reasons given in Ezekiel 35 for the judgment to come to Mount Seir?

Look back at page 162 and note what you learned about Edom when studying Ezekiel 25:12-14.

What do you learn about Edom from Genesis 36:6-8 and Joshua 24:4?

There is much history behind the hatred of Edom toward Israel. Read Numbers 20:14-21 and summarize what happened when Moses wanted to journey through Edom to lead the Israelites to the Promised Land.

"Jacob I have loved; but Esau I have hated, and laid waste his mountains and his heritage for the jackals of the wilderness." (Malachi 1:2,3) This is one of the mysteries of our sovereign Lord. He chose Jacob over Esau. He chose Israel over every other nation. But in choosing Israel, He demonstrated the character of His faithful love even when they were unfaithful. Through His love to Israel, the whole world has an opportunity to see how great God is.

Is the book of Ezekiel about Israel or about the Lord? Please explain your answer.

Did you take time to consider that question? I hope so! What's the phrase that is repeated over and over by the Lord throughout the book of Ezekiel? What's the name of this study? The ultimate in all of eternity is knowing the Lord. When you know Him, you can't help but glorify Him because He is absolutely worthy of glory and honor and praise. Life is not about me. I need to be reminded of that regularly. Coming face-to-face with the sovereignty of our Lord God Almighty humbles me.

The Israelites were now in a position to be humbled and to be in awe of what the Lord was going to do on their behalf. Despite their stiff-necked, hard-hearted rebelliousness toward the Lord throughout their years as a nation, the Lord did not break His covenant with them.

Read Ezekiel 36:1-15 again and make notes of what you learn below.

Reasons for judgment against Edom:

Blessings on Israel:

Look at Ezekiel 36:8. What does the Lord say regarding the return of His people?

The exiles in Babylon should have been excited by these words! This prophecy was partially fulfilled when the exiles were led back to Israel by Zerubbabel under the edict of Cyrus King of Persia. But the history of the nation after that return proves that the rest of the prophecy seen in this chapter, as well as what we read about in Ezekiel 34, has not yet been fulfilled.

What specific promises were given in Ezekiel 36:15?

It didn't take long for the exiles who returned to the land of Israel to realize that the prophecies of the Lord were only partially being fulfilled. You can read about the taunting that Nehemiah and the wall-builders received from Sanballat the Samarian and Tobiah the Ammonite in Nehemiah 4:1-5.

Prophecy has been described as a series of mountain ranges. As you look out at the view, you see the peaks of many mountains, but the distance between them is hard to calculate, and the valleys in between the mountain peaks are not visible at all. Prophecy often describes the great crests of the mountains all at the same time, and doesn't offer comments on the timing or events that will occur in between them. Keep this in mind as we continue studying.

Warren Wiersbe's commentary on Ezekiel describes Chapter 36:1-15 as the restoration and healing of the land. He says:

> Ezekiel described that future day when the land would be healed and once again produce abundant flocks, herds, and harvests. Since the founding of the nation of Israel in 1948, great progress has been made by the Jewish people in reclaiming the land. There has been a great deal of reforestation and irrigation, and the waste places are being transformed. As wonderful as this is, it is nothing compared with what the Lord will do when His people are gathered back to their land from the nations of the world.[4]

We've just begun to grasp the messages of hope that the Lord spoke to the exiles through Ezekiel. Next week we will learn about heart transplants and resurrected bones as well as two baffling battle scenes. Ezekiel is still quite an intriguing preacher!

Reviewing the Revelations

Unit Nine

A Change for the Better

Ezekiel 33—36:15

What were the most meaningful Scriptures or truths from this unit's lessons?

How do these truths impact your daily life?

Is there anything that you have questions about?

Prayer Requests and Praises

Today's Date:

My personal request:

Confidential requests from my friends:

The God of Israel Himself gives strength and power to the people.
Psalm 68:35

Notes

UNIT TEN
Medical and Military Operations

LESSON ONE
A Heart Transplant
EZEKIEL 36:16-38

LESSON TWO
Reconstructive Prophecy
EZEKIEL 37:1-14

LESSON THREE
National Unity
EZEKIEL 37:15-38

LESSON FOUR
The Army of Gog
EZEKIEL 38 and 39

LESSON ONE   *A Heart Transplant*   EZEKIEL 36:16-38

Pray that the Spirit will open your eyes to the timeless truths of the Word of the Lord today and give you a heart of worship.

יהוה

In this unit, we will study what are probably two of the most well-known passages in Ezekiel. In today's lesson we will study the reason that the Lord says He will give Israel a new heart.

"Moreover, the word of the Lord came to me, saying:......"

"I will give you a new heart and put a new spirit within you; I will take the heart of stone out of your flesh, and give you a heart of flesh."   Ezekiel 36:16, 26

Do you remember the first time the Lord said this to Ezekiel? We studied it in Ezekiel 11, back in Unit Three, Lesson Four. If you have accepted Jesus Christ as your Lord and Savior, then you have already undergone a heart transplant. Your cold, hard rebellious heart was circumcised, and you were given a brand new heart. You can look back at our previous study for a review.

In Ezekiel 36:26, the Lord repeats the exact same words that He said in Chapter 11. The context has changed though, and in this chapter the Lord explains to Ezekiel the reason for His incredible plan.

Please read Ezekiel 36:16-38.

Today's best doctors cannot always determine the cause of illnesses, but the Great Physician can. The Lord clearly explains the actions and attitudes of the Israelites and their impact on the world around them.

Follow the explanation of the Lord through the many connective words He uses. Note what He says in the verses below.

Ezekiel 36:17: **When** _____

           They _____

Ezekiel 36:18: **Therefore** _____

           For _____

           For _____

Ezekiel 36:19: ***So*** _____

    And _____

Ezekiel 36:20: ***When*** _____

    They _____

That's the initial diagnosis of the problem. Then the Lord utters a word that changes the course of history. One little word.

Ezekiel 36:21: ***But*** _____

Ezekiel 36:22: ***Therefore*** _____

Ezekiel 36:23: ***And*** _____

    And _____

    When _____

The heart of man was made to worship the Lord. The first commandment to the Israelites was to love the Lord their God with all their heart and soul and strength. But they could not, and we can not, unless there is a change of heart.

Everything that the Lord is about to prescribe and carry out in the next verses is for His name's sake.

Ezekiel 36:24: ***For*** _____

Ezekiel 36:25: ***Then I will*** _____

    And you shall be _____

    I will _____

Ezekiel 36:26: ***I will*** _____

    And _____

    I will _____

    And _____

Does it surprise you that the reason the Lord gives Israel a new heart is for His own sake?

What do you learn about the name of the Lord according to the following verses?

Exodus 20:7

Leviticus 19:12

Are you as reverential toward the name of the Lord as He desires that you be? Take time for a little self-examination. Is there any way that you are profaning the name of the Lord?

After the transplant, the symptoms of the diseased heart are gone, and the nation of Israel can live a healthy, holy life.

Ezekiel 36:27: *I will* _____

And _____

And _____

Ezekiel 36:28: *Then* _____

When the Lord is hallowed in the Israelites' eyes, what difference does it make in their lives? List from Ezekiel 36:28-38 the blessings that the Lord promises to give His people when He gives them a new heart.

There are a few statements in the passage that we have been studying that may be surprising. It is easy to focus on the blessings and the incredible change of heart that the Lord is going to give the Israelites. But in the midst of those exciting promises, the Lord makes a sobering statement.

What does He communicate to the Israelites in Ezekiel 36:31-32?

The change of heart, the pouring out of the Spirit, and the grieving over sin is also described in Zechariah 12:10-13. What else do you learn from this cross-reference?

A day is coming when this prophecy will be fulfilled. The Israelites as a nation have not yet recognized their Savior. But for those of you who have seen Him, have you grieved over your sins against Him? Have you mourned for Him whom you pierced?

We have so great a salvation! But we received it only on the basis of Who the Lord is, not on the basis of who we are.

Read 1 Timothy 1:13-15. Consider how the apostle Paul viewed himself, then write a brief description of yourself.

Humility. Thankfulness. Joy. A healthy heart beats with these. Turn your heart to praise and worship the Lord as He rightly deserves.

Our Father, Who art in heaven, Hallowed be Thy Name.

LESSON TWO *Reconstructive Prophecy* **EZEKIEL** 37:1-14

Ask the Lord to place His hand upon you today as you study His word and seek to follow Him.

𐤉𐤄𐤅𐤄

Today is the day! Have you been wondering through this whole study when we would ever get to that captivating chapter about "dem bones"? I think you will be a little surprised, as I was, that this intriguing illustration is explained in just 14 verses. And then the Lord moves on with another hands-on demonstration for Ezekiel to give to his audience.

Before we actually read the text, I wonder what you know already know about "dem dry bones." Anything? Everything? Jot down a few thoughts…

Now please read Ezekiel 37:1-14.

What happened to Ezekiel? Look at Ezekiel 37:1 and review Ezekiel 1:3, 3:22 and 8:1-3 as you answer this question.

List everything you can learn about the bones described in Ezekiel 37:1-2.

That the bones are "very dry" is a critical point. Instead of being buried, as was the traditional Jewish custom, the bones had been exposed.

◆◆◆◆◆◆◆◆◆◆◆◆◆◆◆◆◆◆◆◆◆◆◆◆◆◆◆◆◆◆◆◆◆◆◆◆◆

Depending upon economic and social status, burial was either in a shallow grave covered with stones or in a cave or tomb hewn out of stone. A tomb was made secure by rolling a circular stone over the entrance and sealing it (Mark 16:3-4). This was done to secure the body from animals. Graves were often marked with a large, upright stone. For a body not to be buried was considered a great shame and a sign of God's judgment (1 Kin. 14:11; 2 Kin. 9:36,37). Unburied bodies polluted the land (Ezek. 39:11–16). [1]

◆◆◆◆◆◆◆◆◆◆◆◆◆◆◆◆◆◆◆◆◆◆◆◆◆◆◆◆◆◆◆◆◆◆◆◆◆

What do you think Ezekiel's initial reaction may have been when he saw the valley with thousands of dry, bleached, brittle bones scattered over the whole area?

What do you learn from the Lord's question and Ezekiel's answer in verse 3? How would you have responded?

The Lord's response to Ezekiel's comment was "Prophesy!" Just picture Ezekiel talking to all those bones. Verse 7 tells us that he didn't hesitate for a moment, "...so I prophesied as I was commanded..." Once again, Ezekiel is an incredible example of an obedient servant of the Lord.

What did the Lord tell Ezekiel to say to the bones? (Ezekiel 37:4-6, notice the verbs and write out each phrase)

We know that Ezekiel prophesied just as he was commanded to do. And then what happened? Look at Ezekiel 37:7.

Please look up the definitions for the following words:
Noise: Strong's #6963
Hebrew word:
Hebrew definition:

Rattling: Strong's #7494
Hebrew word:
Hebrew definition:

In your own words, how would you describe what Ezekiel experienced?

Ezekiel 37:8 points out a very critical detail and sets the stage for Ezekiel's next prophecy. How was the fulfillment of the prophecy in verses 4-6 not completed?

Do you realize at this point, as Ezekiel looks out over the valley, he is no longer looking at scattered bones, but he sees lifeless bodies lying throughout the valley?

What happens in Ezekiel 37:9-10?

Please look up the definition for the following word:
Breath: Strong's #7307
Hebrew word:
Hebrew definition:

The key to interpreting this passage is the next passage. The Lord Himself explains the vision to Ezekiel and to us. Read Ezekiel 37:11-14 and answer the questions below.

What do the bones represent?

What is their situation?

What does the Lord say to them?

Why does He bring them to Israel?

What is His promise in verse 14?

Doesn't the Lord's explanation make everything perfectly clear? Yes! And no! This prophetic passage has been interpreted in a variety of ways. We are studying the Word of God to learn what the author intended to communicate when he wrote it, and to learn what the Lord wants to communicate through that author. We have to study this passage in the context of the surrounding verses, chapters, and the whole book of Ezekiel.

I hope you've come to understand that this book is about the Lord's relationship with His chosen people Israel, the sin they committed against Him, the judgment they deserved, and the restoration of the nation as the people of the Lord. It is very important to realize that the vision of the dry bones coming to life is given in the midst of other prophecies regarding the restoration of the nation of Israel.

The Lord clearly said that "these bones are the whole house of Israel." That is a simple, clear statement, given to Ezekiel as an explanation of the vision. That explanation presents the vision as another way that the Lord is communicating His promise to restore the nation. It is parallel to the previous chapters and those that follow. That "these bones are the whole house of Israel" also tells us, therefore, that the dry bones do not represent individual Israelites, nor do the dry bones represent the resurrection of the body of a believer at the time of rapture.

But what about the "graves" referred to in Ezekiel 37:12,13?

Look at the following verses and note the places — the "graves" from which the Lord will bring His people.

Ezekiel 28:25

Ezekiel 34:13

Ezekiel 36:24

Ezekiel 37:21 (note that this is in the same chapter as the vision of the dry bones)

Has this prophecy been fulfilled? Yes. And no. Under an edict by Cyrus, King of Persia, the Israelite exiles in Babylon began to return to their own land. Then Darius the Mede encouraged more of the people to return to Israel. Finally, King Artexerxes authorized Nehemiah to lead many of the exiles back home. Yet this return to their homeland was not permanent. The little strip of land bordered by the Mediterranean Sea and the Sahara Desert, between Egypt and Europe, has been the place of one military campaign after another. Nation after nation has tried to establish itself there. From AD 70 until 1948, the Israelites had almost no residence in their land whatsoever.

> May 14, 1948, David Ben Gurion addresses the National Council to proclaim the re-birth of the Nation of Israel… "By virtue of the national and historical right of the Jewish people and of the resolution of the General Assembly of the United Nations, we hereby proclaim the establishment of the Jewish State in Palestine, to be called Israel."[2]

Was 1948 the year that the dry bones were gathered from all ends of the earth? Perhaps it was the beginning of the gathering, but it was not the complete fulfillment of this prophecy. There is so much more to come!

In tomorrow's study, we will look at the rest of Chapter 37, and compare the prophecies regarding the restoration of the nation of Israel. As we close today, let's think about how what we've seen today impacts our lives.

We've seen the Lord lay His hand upon Ezekiel and give him a message. Could that happen to you?

We've seen Ezekiel's immediate obedience to the Lord's commands, even though they were quite strange. How obedient are you to the Lord?

We've seen a desperate situation, envisioned as dry bones that appear to have no hope of resuscitation. We've seen a nation that has been destroyed, cut off, scattered, made homeless. But nothing is too difficult for the Lord. Are you facing a situation that seems hopeless? Does change, restoration or refreshment seem not only improbable, but impossible?

May the plan of the Lord for Israel and the power of the Lord over desperation give you hope today for whatever you are facing in your life. His power is made perfect in weakness. One day in the future, you will look back. "'Then you shall know that I, the Lord, have spoken it and performed it,' says the Lord."

LESSON THREE   *National Unity*   EZEKIEL 37:15-28

Take a moment to bow in reverence and adoration of your great Savior-King.

𐤉𐤄𐤅𐤄

The kingdom of God on earth! No one has been looking forward to that day more than the nation of Israel. God intended that the nation of Israel demonstrate to all people how glorious it can be to live under the government of God.[3] But they didn't. And for His name's sake, He judged His people. But also for His name's sake, He promised to renew His people with His Spirit, restore them as a nation, and return them to the Promised Land. When the Israelites were last in their homeland, they were living as a divided people. Two kingdoms. North and South. Israel and Judah. Things will be different when they return.

Read Ezekiel 37:15-23.

Do what Ezekiel did. Draw two sticks and label them as the Lord told him to do.

Now draw them according to Ezekiel 37:17.

Why did the Lord tell Ezekiel to do this? What was the explanation of this demonstration according to Ezekiel 37:21-23?

The next verses will prepare us for the end of the book, Ezekiel 40-48. Please read Ezekiel 37:24-28. This passage excites me so!

What do you learn about the following:

The king:

The people:

The covenant:

The tabernacle:

The Lord:

Throughout His words to Ezekiel, the Lord has given indications of His plan to put a Righteous King on the throne to govern His people. The Lord made a covenant with David. Let's trace the promise through the pages of Scripture. Note what is said in the following verses:

2 Samuel 7:8-13

Isaiah 9:6,7

Jeremiah 30:9

Hosea 3:4-5

Micah 5:2-5

Luke 1:31-33

Revelation 22:16

> David, King of Israel had been dead upwards of 400 years; and from that time till now there never has been a ruler of any kind in the Jewish nation of the name of David. By David, then, we must understand the Messiah, as the Jews themselves acknowledge, so called because He is descended from him, and also is the well beloved, Son of the Father, as the name imports, and in whom all the promises made to David were fulfilled. [4]

"We have found the Messiah, (which is translated, the Christ)

And he brought him to Jesus." John 1:41-42

Our Jesus, who was born in Bethlehem, who lived and walked among us 2000 years ago, who loved us and gave Himself for us, who died, was buried, and rose on the third day, our Jesus, is the Messiah, the Anointed, the seed of David! Our Jesus is the One King! He is the One Shepherd who will feed, shepherd, and reign over the nation of Israel when they are restored in the Promised Land.

I need a new song to sing to Him! But it is the Lord who will be singing a new song! Turn to Zephaniah 3:14-17 and rejoice with His people and with Him. Record your praise below.

Let's review the prophecies that the Lord has given to Ezekiel in the last few chapters. We'll come away with a summary of the glorious future that awaits the nation of Israel. Fill in the chart on the next page. The categories are just guidelines, some may not apply.

Prophecies	Ezekiel 34:11-31	Ezekiel 36:26-38	Ezekiel 37:11-28
Will be gathered from			
Will be brought to			
Blessings on the land			
Changes in the people			
Blessings on the people			
Relationship with the Lord			
Reputation of the Lord			
Reputation of the people			
Blessings on the nation			
Details of the covenant			

In the previous chart, you created a description of the Millennial Kingdom. The nation of Israel will enjoy the reign of Jesus Christ, the Messiah-King, on earth for 1,000 years. Do you remember from Day One of this week that the Lord is restoring Israel for His Name's sake? The blessings on Israel will give glory to the Lord.

God is most glorified when we are most satisfied in Him.[5]

John Piper

Are you satisfied in the Lord? Why or why not?

"This people I have formed for Myself; They shall declare My praise." Isaiah 43:21 You don't have to wait to praise Him. He has already restored you to Himself, He has already changed your heart and given you His Spirit. He has already made you a citizen of heaven with all the saints. You are already a servant of the King of Kings and you know Him as your Good Shepherd. You are His sanctuary, His dwelling place. He is in your midst. And He will be with you always, even until the end of the age. Praise Him!

LESSON FOUR *The Army of Gog* **EZEKIEL** 38 and 39

Pray that you will trust the Lord for His victory in your life.

יהוה

What an exciting week of study we have had! I hope you've gained an understanding of the Lord's incredible promises for His people. We will finish this week with another mind-boggling prophecy. I don't think anyone has come to a completely accurate understanding of the events we are about to read about, and we probably won't either. But we will see the Lord in His power and glory, and that's good enough for me. The Lord seems to want to keep some things mysterious. He has the right to do so.

I'm going to give you a little geography lesson before you even begin reading. Hopefully it will help you as you take in the prophesied attack on Israel. The names of the places that you will read about are first mentioned in Genesis 10:2 in the geneology of Japheth son of Noah: "The sons of Japheth were Gomer, Magog, Madia, Javan, Tubal, Meschech, and Tiras." The geographical locations were named according to Japheth's sons who established communities there.

In Ezekiel 38 and 39:

Gog — *the one to whom the prophecy is spoken against, the prince of the land of Magog. The title was probably a common one of the kings of the country, like "Pharoah" in Egypt.[6] Gog was also the prince over the lands of Rosh, Meshech, and Tubal.*

Magog — *the land to the north of Israel from which the army comes*

Rosh — *probably modern day Russia*

Meshech *and* ***Tubal*** — *geographical areas in eastern Asia Minor (modern day Turkey)*

Persia — *modern Iran*

Ethiopia — *in Hebrew called Cush, this is ancient Ethiopia, modern Sudan and Ethiopia*

Libya — *in Hebrew called Put; this is modern Libya*

Gomer *and* ***Togarmah*** — *located in eastern Asia Minor (modern day Turkey)*

I hope that helps you get through the first six verses of the chapter! We will be reading Ezekiel 38 and 39. You may read through it all at one sitting and then answer the questions below, or read it according to the passages given below.

Please read Ezekiel 38:1-9. What do you learn from verse 8 that relates this passage to the previous chapters (Ezekiel 34, 35, 36, 37)?

Read Ezekiel 38:10-13. What is Gog's evil plan?

Ezekiel 38:11 gives a description of the land of Israel that gives us a clue to the timing of this attack. What do we learn about the nation of Israel at this time?

Peace in Israel. Can you imagine it? According to Daniel 9:27, there will come a day when the nation of Israel will enter into a covenant with a world leader; that covenant will guarantee peace, safety, and protection. It is during this time that Gog's army will plan to attack Israel.

Warren Wiersbe presents this suggested scenario:

1. Rapture (1 Thessalonians 4:13-18)

2. Israel covenants with 10-nation European coalition for seven years to build temple. (This begins the period of time known as the Tribulation.)

- *Peace in Israel for 3 ½ years*

- *After 3 ½ years, the leader of the coalition emerges as the Antichrist and breaks the covenant. He sets up his own image in the temple, and tries to force the world to worship him. (Dan. 9:27; 2 Thess. 2:1-12; Matt.24:15; Rev. 13)*

- *Wrath of God experienced for 3 ½ years*

3. Christ returns to earth to defeat Satan and the Beast and establish His kingdom. (At this time the Battle of Armageddon is fought.) Rev. 19:11-20:6 [7]

After reading through the rest of Ezekiel 38 and 39, we will compare this battle to the battle of Armageddon. There are many differences which seem to indicate two separate large scale military operations.

Read Ezekiel 38:14-17. How is the attack described?

Who is actually directing the movements of this army? _____

Read Ezekiel 38:18-23. What will happen "when Gog comes against the land of Israel"? (List everything that you see.)

What is the purpose of this outpouring of the wrath of the Lord against Gog's armies?

Read Ezekiel 39:1-8. What additional details are given regarding the destruction of Gog's armies?

What does the Lord plan to accomplish through the defeat of this vast army?

Read Ezekiel 39:9-16. What is the situation after the defeat of the army? What is done about it? Note the times mentioned and the special workforce created.

Read Ezekiel 39:17-20. Who does Ezekiel speak to now? What does he invite them to do?

Let's take a little time now and compare this battle to the battles described in Revelation. Did you realize that there are three major end-time world wars? The attack from Gog during a time of peace, the battle at Armageddon, and the final rebellion after the millennial reign of Christ. There are similarities between these three battles, but there are obvious contrasts as well. I'll summarize Ezekiel's description, and you fill in the blanks for the description of the battles in Revelation.

Regarding the leader of the army:

Attack from Gog Ezekiel 38:7, 12 — **Gog leads the coalition to attack Israel**

Battle at Armegeddon Revelation 19:19 — _____

Final Rebellion Revelation 20:7,8 — _____

Regarding the members of the army:

Attack from Gog Ezekiel 38:6,15;39:2 — **A coalition of at least eight nations surrounding Israel invading from the north**

Battle at Armageddon Revelation 16:14,16; Rev. 19:19 — _____

Final Rebellion Revelation 20:7-8 — _____

Regarding how the army is destroyed:

Attack from Gog Ezekiel 39:17-23 — **Gog's armies are attacked with pestilence, hailstones, brimstone, and the armies fight each other**

Battle at Armageddon Revelation 19:19-21 — _____

Final Rebellion Revelation 20:9 — _____

Regarding the aftermath of the war:

Attack from Gog Ezekiel 39:12 — **The people of Israel spend seven months burying corpses from Gog's invasion**

Battle at Armageddon Revelation 19:17-18 — _____

Final Rebellion Revelation 20:9 — _____

Well, what do you think?!? I mentioned at the beginning of this lesson that there is not a consensus on the correct interpretation of these passages. I obviously see Scriptures which lead me to think that there are three extraordinary end-time wars. Perhaps there are only two. We can speculate but still trust that the Lord knows exactly what the future holds. And what is most important is that He is the victor of each battle, whether there is one or two or three.

History is the final interpreter of prophecy, for as Jesus said, "I am telling you now before it happens, so that when it does happen you will believe that I am He." [8]

Read Ezekiel 39:21-29. This is a beautiful conclusion to the prophecy regarding the attack from Gog.

The Lord once again gives the reason for the judgment against Israel and reviews the promises that He has made to them. List each promise given in the following verses:

Ezekiel 39:21

Ezekiel 39:22

Ezekiel 39:25

Ezekiel 39:27

Ezekiel 39:28

Ezekiel 39:29

These promises are magnificent. I hope that you are recognizing that when the Lord has a plan, He sticks to it. He keeps His promises. And He makes it very clear why He does so.

I have highlighted the verses below in my Bible; I encourage you to do the same. Read them and summarize the priority of the Lord.

Ezekiel 38:16, 23

Ezekiel 39:6b, 7b, 22, 28

Isaiah 59:19-21

Many chapters ago, we looked at a comment that the Israelites were making. It had even become a proverb: "The days are prolonged, and every vision fails." Ezekiel 12:22 Because the Lord had not already judged them for their idolatry and rebellion, they thought He never would. But the delay in judgment did not mean the elimination of judgment. And now, the delay in the Lord's gathering of His people does not mean that He will not gather them. The Lord's timing is perfect. He carries out His plan when the fullness of the time is right.

Are you waiting on the Lord for something? Will you trust Him for His perfect timing?

I'd like to draw your attention to a promise from the Lord spoken through the apostle Paul. I think it is a beautiful New Testament parallel to Ezekiel 38 and 39.

Read Romans 8:31-39 and list the promises for those who are in Christ.

When you think of the mysterious army of Gog and how it will one day come against Israel, think of this verse. The army of Gog versus the army of God. If God is for us, then who can be against us? No matter what type of enemy you face, the Lord is for you, and the battle belongs to Him.

Reviewing the Revelations

Unit Ten

Medical and Military Operations

Ezekiel 36:16—39

What were the most meaningful Scriptures or truths from this unit's lessons?

How do these truths impact your daily life?

Is there anything that you have questions about?

Prayer Requests and Praises

Today's Date:

My personal request:

Confidential requests from my friends:

Be persistent in your prayers for all Christians everywhere....
Ephesians 6:18   NLT

Notes

UNIT ELEVEN

Great Expectations

LESSON ONE
A Blueprint for Blessings
Ezekiel 40–42

LESSON TWO
The Return of the Lord
EZEKIEL 43:1-9

LESSON THREE
Sacrifices to the Savior
EZEKIEL 43:10-27

LESSON FOUR
Good and Faithful Servants
EZEKIEL 44:1-31

LESSON ONE — *Blueprints of Blessings* — EZEKIEL 40-42

Please pray that you will "be diligent to present yourself approved unto God, a student unashamed, rightly dividing the word of truth."

𐤉𐤄𐤅𐤄

Anticipation! Expectation! Yearning! Eagerness! The next eight chapters in Ezekiel should create an overwhelming sense of these feelings! The promises that we are about to study have incredibly deep meaning for the nation of Israel, and I trust that the Lord will show us what they are to mean to us as well. Please read the following excerpt from John MacArthur's Study Bible notes:

> ...this section provides explicit details concerning Christ's millennial reign... giving more detail about the 1,000 year kingdom than all other OT prophecies put together. It is the "holy of holies" among millennial forecasts. As has been done with the previous 39 chapters, this concluding portion will also be approached in a literal, historical manner which best serves the interpreter in all Scripture. In many ways these chapters are the most important in the book since they form the crowning reality, the climax of Ezekiel's prophecy and Israel's restoration. The section includes: 1) the new temple (40:1–43:12); 2) the new worship (43:13–46:24); and 3) the new apportionment of the Land (47:1–48:35).[1]

The "holy of holies" among millennial forecasts! The vision shown by the Lord in Ezekiel 40—48 is incredible. But I'm afraid that many come to these chapters and get bogged down in the details. We come without a Jewish background, without an appreciation for worship in the temple, without an understanding of the signifigance of the divisions of the Promised Land.

In spite of our cultural handicaps, let's study these magnificent chapters with the perspective that if the Lord loves the nation of Israel, then so should we. His plans for their future are important enough to be recorded in His eternal word. Rejoice with those who rejoice!

You are about to encounter many specific measurements given in cubits and handbreadths, and you will see that a rod was used for measuring rather than the yardstick that we use today. You do not have to calculate measurements as you read these passages! But here is some information that may be helpful. A cubit was about 18 inches, or the distance from the fingertips to the elbow. A handbreadth was about three inches, or the width of the hand across its widest part. The length of the rod was determined based on cubits and handbreadth: the rod used in these verses was about 10.5 feet.[2]

Please read Ezekiel 40:1-49.

What stood out to you as you read this chapter?

Let's ask a few important questions of the text. According to Ezekiel 40:1-4:

When does this vision happen?

Who is involved in the vision?

Where does this take place?

What instruction is given?

One of the key words in this chapter, as well as in Chapters 41 and 42, is "measured." What is being measured in the following verses? You do not have to list the measurements, just that which is being measured, i.e. the eastern gateway – Ezekiel 40:6

Ezekiel 40:5	**Ezekiel 40:28**
Ezekiel 40:6	**Ezekiel 40:32**
Ezekiel 40:17-19	**Ezekiel 40:35**
Ezekiel 40:20	**Ezekiel 40:47**
Ezekiel 40:24	

In this chapter, Ezekiel is given a tour of the temple grounds. His guide takes him from one location to the other, measuring each feature of the temple.

Looking at your list above mark on the following diagram the movement of Ezekiel. You can number each of his stops, #1, #2, #3, and use arrows to show the direction that he was led in. (Notice that the diagrams have been turned, so that the eastern gateways actually face south in the pictures.) Make any other notes on the diagram that would be helpful to you to envision the details of the temple.

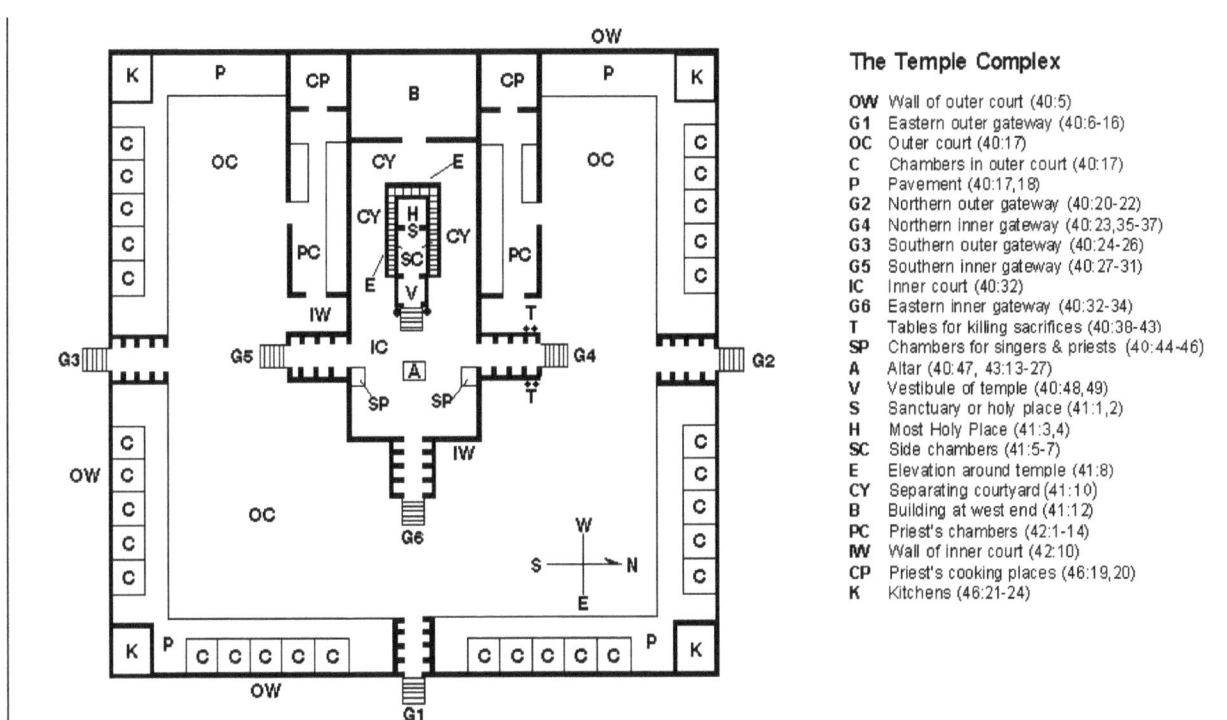

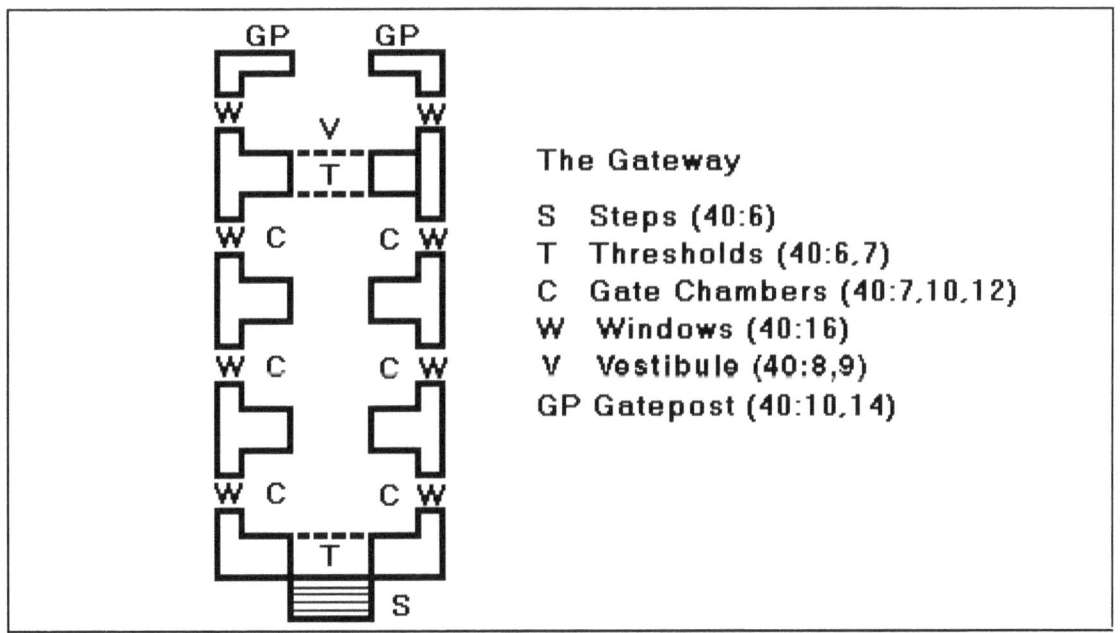

Read Ezekiel 41:1-26 and then Ezekiel 42:1-20, continuing to observe the movement of Ezekiel around the temple grounds. This is to give you an overview of these chapters.

I want you to understand that the intricacy of the details given here are critical to the interpretation of these chapters. Ezekiel recorded a clear description of features, locations, heights and widths. This is a description of a literal temple. Even though the particulars are difficult for us to envision, we must realize that they are part of the inspired Word of God. The day will come when these descriptions will no longer be seen through the eyes of faith, but will be seen through our very own eyes. We will be able to tour the temple grounds ourselves!

Turn back to page 55 and look through the last tour that Ezekiel was given through the temple.

One thing I have desired of the Lord, that will I seek: that I may dwell in the house of the Lord all the days of my life, to behold the beauty of the Lord, and to inquire in His temple..   Psalm 27:4 NKJV

How would you describe your desire to be in the presence of the Lord?

The most breathtaking aspect of this temple is that it is the complete fulfillment of the Lord's desire to dwell with His people.

What did the Lord communicate in the following verses?

Exodus 25:8

Levitcus 26:11-12

Look up the definition for the following words:
Sanctuary: Strong's #4720
Hebrew word:
Hebrew definition:

Dwell: Strong's #7931
Hebrew word:
Hebrew definition:

Remember that Ezekiel had been in training to be a priest. He would have been intimately acquainted with the temple. He had lived in Israel and had probably spent time in the magnificent temple built by Solomon. After being exiled, the Lord took him back to the temple in a vision, and he was shown the horrible idolatry committed by the people and the priests. We studied this in Week Three. Before that vision ended, Ezekiel saw something shocking.

What happened in Ezekiel 10:18-19 and Ezekiel 11:23?

Since that time, the nation of Israel has been waiting for the return of the Lord. The disciple John tells us that "the Word became flesh and dwelt among us, and we beheld His glory, the glory as of the only begotten of the Father, full of grace and truth." John 1:14 The Lord returned to Israel in the flesh, but the nation of Israel as a whole did not recognize Him. They are still waiting for His return. Until the Lord returns to dwell in the future glorious temple that He has planned, He dwells in each believer in Jesus Christ.

Record the truth stated in 1 Corinthians 6:19-20.

This is an astonishing truth! The millennial temple will be breathtaking, but it takes my breath away that the Lord dwells in me today!

LESSON TWO — *The Return of the Lord* — EZEKIEL 43:1-9

Enter the courts of the Lord today with praise and thanksgiving to Him for being your God.

יהוה

On the Fourth of July, my family often attends our state symphony's concert and fireworks show. As the patriotic salute crescendos, I anticipate the grand finale in the song and in the sky. Incredible bursts of color and light, crashing cymbals and pounding drums lead me to think – this is it! But the show continues. Multiple booms from the fireworks and an even greater crescendo in the music lead me again to think – this is it. And the show still continues! The grand finale is always spectacular and always a surprise!

The Lord's plans for the end times are much more spectacular than a Fourth of July fireworks display, of course. But, there are many extravagant events that lead me to think – this is it! This is the greatest thing that will happen! But the extraordinary must be the ordinary in the end! The grand finale never is! Today we will look at just one of the extraordinary anticipated events of the end times.

We've already experienced the fanfare in Ezekiel 40, 41, and 42. May we have a drumroll please?

Read Ezekiel 43:1-9. Write your own symphony of praise and describe what Ezekiel saw.

How did Ezekiel respond to what he saw?

The key repeated words in Ezekiel 43:1-5 are "gate," "east" and "glory." Why are these words important?

Look ahead to Ezekiel 44:1-2 to see additional importance to the words above.

Do you remember the vision that Ezekiel saw when he was by the River Chebar? Turn back to Ezekiel 1:26-28 and slowly take in the vision of the glory of the Lord. Imagine seeing the Lord returning to Israel, to the perfect millennial temple. Note below your thoughts and reflections about this event.

Is this the grand finale? It seems like it could be! Jesus Christ returns to the earth, stands on the Mount of Olives, the earth shakes and splits, and the Temple Mount becomes the high mountain in which all nations will come to worship the Lord. Jesus Christ in all of His glory enters through the East Gate of the Temple and takes His place as Shepherd-King and Great High Priest among His people.

*But this is **not** the grand finale! It's the prelude to the long-awaited Kingdom of Heaven on earth. When Jesus returns and the Israelites look on Him whom they have pierced, when they mourn, repent, and worship Him, the Millennial Kingdom – Christ's one thousand year reign on earth – is just beginning.*

Now that you know that the Lord will be there, I think you will have a better appreciation for some of the features of the temple that were shown to Ezekiel.

What areas were shown to Ezekiel in the following verses?

Ezekiel 40:17

Ezekiel 40:28

Ezekiel 40:35

Ezekiel 40:38-39

Ezekiel 40:47b

Ezekiel 41:1-4

Ezekiel 42:13-14

*From our previous tour through the temple and the exercise above, you should have a good idea of what spaces and furnishings are a part of the millennial temple. There are several features of the wilderness tabernacle, Solomon's temple, and Herod's temple that are **not** mentioned. Remember Ezekiel 43:1-9 as you consider the following questions.*

There will be no wall of separation in the outer court between the Jews and the Gentiles as there was at Herod's temple. Why not? See Ephesians 2:14-18.

No golden lampstand is mentioned. Why not? See Exodus 25:31,37; Isaiah 60:19; John 8:12.

No altar of incense is mentioned. Why not? See Exodus 30:1,8; Psalm 141:2; Revelation 8:3.

No veil between the holy place and the holy of holies is mentioned. Why not? See Mark 15:38 and Hebrews 10:19-22.

No ark of the covenant is mentioned. Why not? See Exodus 25:21-22, Isaiah 2:1-3, Jeremiah 3:16-17, Hebrews 4:16.

The pattern of worship which was given to Moses in the wilderness was only a shadow of heavenly things. Each of the furnishings symbolized Christ and our relationship with Him in some way. Although much will change regarding the Israelites' worship of the Lord, they will still practice one aspect of that which was prescribed in levitical law.

Look back at the previous exercise in which you listed features of the millennial temple. From these descriptions, what would you expect to be a part of Israel's worship of the Lord during His millennial reign?

Read Ezekiel 43:10-27. What do you think are two key words in this passage? You should see a special emphasis on how the Israelites will worship the Lord in this temple. We will learn more about these practices tomorrow.

Our studies this week focus on the Israelites' future worship of the Lord. The Lord is waiting and anticipating their whole-hearted worship. He is administrating the events of history to bring them to Himself. How has the Lord administrated, managed or directed the events of your life to bring you to Himself?

The Lord wants whole-hearted worship from you now. Are you holding anything back? How are you worshipping Him today?

LESSON THREE — *Sacrifices to the Savior* — EZEKIEL 43:10-27

Please pray that the Holy Spirit will lead you to a deeper understanding and appreciation for the sacrifice that Jesus Christ made for you.

𐤉𐤄𐤅𐤄

We are in the midst of contemplating the future. It's often hard to understand our present day and why the Lord allows things to be the way they are, so it shouldn't surprise us that we find it hard to fully comprehend the Lord's plans for the future. The previous lesson should have highlighted the truth from Scripture that the Millennial Temple will have an altar on which sacrifices and offerings will be made to the Lord. This truth is one that many have used as an argument against these chapters (Ezekiel 40 — 48) as being literal, actual, future reality. You may have already wondered: "Why will there be animal sacrifices and offerings in the Temple since Jesus was the one perfect offering for all time?" I hope our lesson today will give you an answer to that question!

In the previous lesson, we looked at Ezekiel 43 in relation to the previous chapters that described the furnishings of the temple. We need to read it again today to gain the proper perspective and context for our consideration of the reason for sacrifices during the Millenial Kingdom.

Please read Ezekiel 43:1-12.

What does the Lord declare in verse 7?

What does He review in verses 8 and 9?

Look very closely at Ezekiel 43:10-11. What cause and effect relationships do you see explained in these verses? Look for words such as: *that... so... if.*

What verbs do you observe in these two verses?

List the phrases in Ezekiel 43:10,11 that include the repeated idea of "all."

How would you summarize the desire of the Lord for His people according to the observations you have just made?

Isn't that what the Lord desired from the very beginning? Record what you observe from the following verses:

Exodus 24:3-4

Numbers 28:2

Deuteronomy 4:39-40

That was the command. However, the Lord knew that His people could not do it. You know they couldn't do it. But they didn't know they couldn't do it. They learned that the hard way. Yet the Lord promised the solution before they fully encountered the problem.

Please slowly read Deuteronomy 30:1-10.

Is this passage as amazing to you as it is to me? It is the Lord's very own prophecy of what we are studying in Ezekiel. How does Deuteronomy 30:8 relate to Ezekiel 43:10-12?

This is a good time to reflect on what you tell the Lord you will do. Why couldn't the Israelites keep the commands of the Lord?

Do you think that you are able to obey the Lord? Why or why not?

Please write out the truth of Galatians 2:20.

That's truth that never grows old. Anytime you start to think: "I can do it...," please remember that Christ alone is your strength. He is your life. Without Him you can do nothing. (John 15:5)

In Ezekiel 43:1-12, the Lord sets the stage for the instructions that He is about to give Ezekiel regarding the altar of sacrifice. The measurements and details for consecrating the altar are given in the rest of the chapter.

Read Ezekiel 43:18-27.

Who is involved in the consecration of the altar?

How long does the consecration last?

Briefly describe the actions that are to be taken.

What are the reasons for the consecration of the altar according to Ezekiel 43:26-27?

Please look up the definition for the following word:
Accepted: Strong's #7521
Hebrew word:
Hebrew definition:

Now look at the following cross-references in which the same word is used and note what you learn.

Ezekiel 20:40-41

Isaiah 40:2 (*ratsah* is translated as "pardoned")

Look back over what you have studied so far in this lesson. How would you summarize the reason for sacrifices being a part of worship in the Millenial Temple based on what we have studied today?

We have been studying the Lord's reasons for sacrifices to be a part of the Israelites' worship. In the book of Romans, the apostle Paul gives us a full explanation of the Lord's plans and purposes regarding His chosen people. Although the nation at present rejects the gospel and rejects their true Messiah, Jesus Christ, the day will come when "all Israel will be saved." (Romans 11:26) After explaining that the Lord will demonstrate His mercy on His people, Paul exuberantly praises the Lord for the depth of the riches both of His wisdom and knowledge. He rejoices that His judgments are unsearchable and His ways are past finding out.

"For who has known the mind of the Lord? Or who has become His counselor? Or who has first given to Him and it shall be repaid to Him? For of Him and through Him and to Him are all things, to whom be glory forever. Amen." Romans 11:34-36

Immediately following his teaching on the Lord's relationship with His people Israel, just after Paul's great praise to the Lord, Paul says to the Roman believers: **Therefore...** *Because of what Paul has explained in the previous chapters, he says: therefore…*

Record the complete instruction from Paul found in Romans 12:1-2.

I hope a few words stood out to you in a new light after today's studies in Ezekiel! Highlight the words "sacrifice" and "acceptable." Even though Jesus Christ made the perfect sacrifice for us, we are still commanded to make sacrifices to the Lord today! One of the ways that we can express the fullness of our love for the Lord is by laying our own lives down on His altar. It's the way Jesus showed the fullness of His love for us.

What sacrifice will you offer the Lord today?

LESSON FOUR — *Good and Faithful Servants* — EZEKIEL 44:1-31

"Take your sandals off your feet, for the place where you stand is holy ground." Exodus 3:5

יהוה

Have you ever visited an impressive religious monument? There have been many temples, sanctuaries, and structures built to honor and worship the gods of various cultures. Most of these structures are now nothing more than tourist sites. While Ezekiel has been given a tour of the great Millennial Temple, the Word of the Lord makes it very clear that this is a holy place and it has a holy purpose. Today we will see that the Lord is also very clear about who will have the privilege of serving Him and who will be allowed to enter His sanctuary.

Please read Ezekiel 44:1-3, then compare it to Ezekiel 40:6.

What is the difference between these two passages and descriptions of the Eastern Gateway?

In Lesson One, you reviewed what Ezekiel had witnessed before the destruction of Jerusalem. The glory of the Lord departed from the temple through the Eastern Gate.

Now look at Ezekiel 43:1-4, 7, 9. What occurred, and what did the Lord declare?

Look carefully at Ezekiel 44:2 – it contains four phrases that emphasize one concept. Repetition indicates importance.

What is the importance of the Eastern gate being shut?

> As a mark of respect to an Eastern monarch, the gate by which he enters is thenceforth shut to all other persons. [4]

The nation of Israel has experienced short-lived stability for most of its existence. The tabernacle was a tent in the wilderness that was packed up and moved through the Exodus journey. There was no permanent place for the house of the Lord until Solomon completed the temple in 961 B.C., but four hundred years later, it was destroyed. In 516 B.C., the temple built under Zerubbabel's supervision was completed, and then around 20 B.C. King Herod began to remodel it. Herod created a grand structure over a period of 46 years, yet six short years after its completion, it was destroyed by the Romans.(AD 70) Since that time, the Jewish Diaspora has packed up and relocated from one territory to another, always struggling to have a home of their own. Even now, the territories in which they live are under negotiation. Things will be different during the Millennial Kingdom! The vision of the temple shown to Ezekiel indicates a permanent dwelling for the Lord, a place where He will live in their midst forever, and they will have a land of their own.

Please read Ezekiel 44:4 slowly, and preferably out loud.

When was the last time that you were moved in such a way by the glory of the Lord?

Seeing the Lord in all of His glory, experiencing His presence on the mountaintop, and knowing Him as your Lord are preparations for you to respond to His call. He prepares us to do His work by showing Himself to us.

Read Ezekiel 44:5-6. What was Ezekiel commanded to do?

Even in the midst of the incredible vision of the future temple, Ezekiel is still given the responsibility of declaring truth to the house of Israel.

Let us "mark well who may enter the house and all who go out from the sanctuary" in the following exercises. Read Ezekiel 44:6-8. What is the point of this passage?

Read Ezekiel 44:10-14. List in the columns below everything that you learn about the Levites from this passage. Also note the contrasts in this passage indicated by words such as "yet," and "nevertheless."

The Levites' Past	The Levites' Future

In contrast to the denigration of the Levites who went astray, we will see that those Levites who followed the Lord will be honored and promoted.

Read Ezekiel 44:15-31.

Very briefly, describe who and what this passage is about.

What repeated concept do you see in Ezekiel 40:46 and Ezekiel 44:15,16?

For one example of the Levites in the past who didn't honor the Lord, read Numbers 16:1-11. What was the privilege of the priests that they "considered a small thing"?

The Kohathites had received specific, special instruction from the Lord regarding their service in the tabernacle. They were the group of priests who were to carry the most holy things from camp to camp. The Kohathites would have transported the golden lampstand, the altar of incense, and the very ark of the covenant! But they weren't satisfied with their role in the tabernacle. They wanted Moses job.

Has the Lord given you a special assignment that you consider to be "a small thing?" Do you secretly desire the position that someone else holds? Please pray through these concerns, and be sobered by the observation that even what you have been given may be taken away.

The Zadokites were different from the Kohathites. They are described in Ezekiel 44:15 and Ezekiel 48:11. What did they do that will cause them to receive an eternal reward?

And it all started with the faithfulness of one. During King David's reign, the Lord raised up a committed servant. Note what you learn about Zadok from the following references:

1 Chronicles 12:23, 28

1 Chronicles 16:37-40

1 Kings 1:39

Have you ever heard of Zadok? I think that he is one of the great unsung heroes! He was more faithful and obedient than most of our favorite Bible characters. I'm sure he wasn't perfect, but he sets a compelling example for us to follow.

Describe the incredible privilege and reward that the Zadokites will receive according to Ezekiel 44:16 and 28.

A look into the New Testament will help us see how we are to be faithful in that to which the Lord has called us. "Who then is a faithful and wise servant, whom his master made ruler over his household, to give them food in due season? Blessed is that servant whom his master, when he comes will find so doing." Matthew 24:45,46

What attitudes and motivations for your ministry do you find in the following verses?

1 Timothy 1:12

1 Peter 4:10-11

1 Corinthians 15:58

Does the example of Zadok and the exhortation in the New Testament encourage you or convict you regarding your attitude and actions in service to the Lord? If so, in what way?

> Blessed is the man You choose, and cause to approach You, that he may dwell in Your courts. We shall be satisfied with the goodness of Your house, of Your holy temple.   Psalm 65:4

We have just seen the incredible vision of the return of the glory of the Lord to His temple. During the culture of Ezekiel's time, measuring property was symbolic of taking ownership of the place,[5] and we have seen that every aspect of the future Millennial temple was measured rod by rod and cubit by cubit! That's a clear indication that the Lord has claimed this temple as His very own dwelling place. He arrived, and shut the door behind Him; He will dwell there forever.

Sacrifices will be offered to Him there, and His people will be shepherded by none other than the Lord's Anointed One – Jesus Christ. The Millennial temple will be a place set apart, holy to the Lord, and His faithful servants will minister to Him there.

There's still more to come in the future of Israel. The final chapters of Ezekiel are as exciting as all that we have studied so far!

Reviewing the Revelations

Unit Eleven

Great Expectations

Ezekiel 40 — 44

What were the most meaningful Scriptures or truths from this unit's lessons?

How do these truths impact your daily life?

Is there anything that you have questions about?

Prayer Requests and Praises

Today's Date:

My personal request:

Confidential requests from my friends:

Be joyful always; pray continually; give thanks in all circumstances, for this is God's will for you. 1 Thessalonians 5:16-18   NIV

Notes

UNIT TWELVE

The Kingdom of Christ

LESSON ONE
The Heart of Worship
EZEKIEL 45—46

LESSON TWO
The River of Life
EZEKIEL 47:1-12

LESSON THREE
The Covenant Fulfilled
EZEKIEL 47:13—48:35

LESSON FOUR
The Lord Is There
EZEKIEL 48:35

LESSON ONE — *The Heart of Worship* — EZEKIEL 45-46

Please pray for wisdom from the Holy Spirit to understand true worship of our holy Lord.

יהוה

We are about to conclude our study of the book of Ezekiel. The Lord spoke to him over a twenty-five year period, and we've only spent a short time absorbing what He said. I hope you are more familiar with the Word of the Lord to Ezekiel, but you probably don't feel like you've mastered it. I certainly don't!

As we come to the final chapters of Ezekiel, I'll prepare you by letting you know that our study really doesn't get any easier! We are still in the midst of studying the written account of Ezekiel's vision of the Millennial Kingdom. It is complex and details topics with which we are not familiar. There are many more measurements to plot, as well as feasts and offerings to understand. But let me entice you with something else to come: the scene of a river flowing through the land: "Along the bank of the river, on this side and that, will grow all kinds of trees used for food; their leaves will not wither, and their fruit will not fail. They will bear fruit every month, because their water flows from the sanctuary." (Ezekiel 47:12) I am looking forward to envisioning the river in our studies!

Today we will concentrate on the instructions for worship of the Holy One of Israel. The first passage that you will read describes a special area in the land of Israel. This area is also described in Ezekiel 48, and we will examine it when we study that chapter.

Please read the following passage and mark, circle, or highlight the word "holy" as well as that which it modifies.

Ezekiel 45

¹ "Moreover, when you divide the land by lot into inheritance, you shall set apart a district for the LORD, a holy section of the land; its length shall be twenty-five thousand cubits, and the width ten thousand. It shall be holy throughout its territory all around. ²Of this there shall be a square plot for the sanctuary, five hundred by five hundred rods, with fifty cubits around it for an open space. ³So this is the district you shall measure: twenty-five thousand cubits long and ten thousand wide; in it shall be the sanctuary, the Most Holy Place. ⁴It shall be a holy section of the land, belonging to the priests, the ministers of the sanctuary, who come near to minister to the LORD; it shall be a place for their houses and a holy place for the sanctuary. ⁵An area twenty-five thousand cubits long and ten thousand wide shall belong to the Levites, the ministers of the temple; they shall have twenty chambers as a possession.

⁶"You shall appoint as the property of the city an area five thousand cubits wide and twenty-five thousand long, adjacent to the district of the holy section; it shall belong to the whole house of Israel.

⁷"The prince shall have a section on one side and the other of the holy district and the city's property; and bordering on the holy district and the city's property, extending westward on the west side and eastward on the east side, the length shall be side by side with one of the tribal portions, from the west border to the east border. ⁸The land shall be his possession in Israel; and My princes shall no more oppress My people, but they shall give the rest of the land to the house of Israel, according to their tribes."

What title would you give this passage of Scripture?

Please read the passage again, and label the following diagram¹ from the description of the holy district. You may want to highlight the measurements in the passage above that correspond to the various sections.

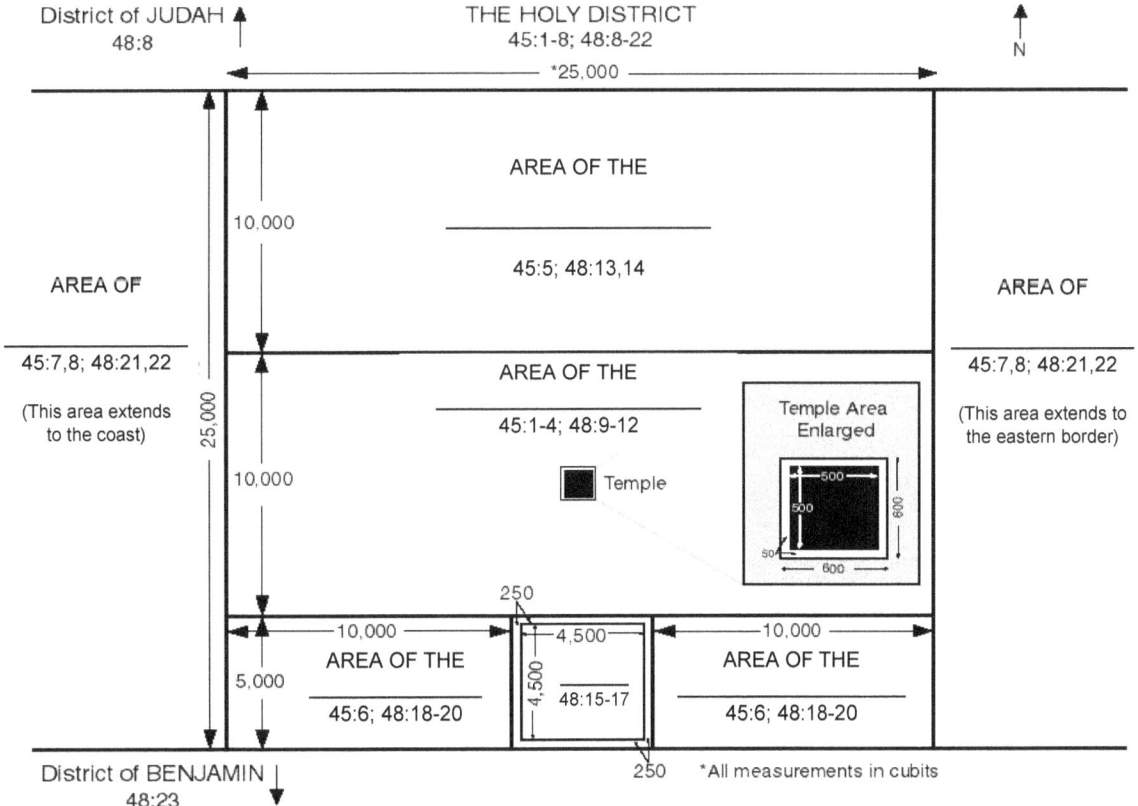

> The prophet was concerned about more than simply assuring the exiles that there would be an equitable reallocation of the land at some point in the future. Ezekiel wanted to reorient his hearers' focus on to what the original idea of a Promised Land was all about: a land in which God would dwell in their midst. [2]

The description of the Holy District follows the description of the conduct for the priests. It then transitions to a description of conduct for the princes, as well as an explanation of their responsibilities.

> Ezekiel introduces "the prince" in 44:1-3 and mentions him at least sixteen times in the rest of the book. He is not to be confused with "David...their prince" (34:24; 37:24-25) whom some see as the Messiah, the heir to David's throne (Luke 1:30-32); nor should he be confused with the Messiah. The prince will be a married man and will have sons who can inherit his land (Ezek. 46:16-18), which is located on either side of the central sacred area. Nowhere is he identified as a member of the royal family, a priest, or a Levite. We aren't even told what tribe he will come from. Apparently he will be a civil ruler, a vice-regent under the authority of the Messiah, and yet most of his functions will be religious. [3]

Please read Ezekiel 45:7-17.

What do you learn about the provisions made for the prince(s)? (Ezekiel 45:7-8)

What do you learn about the conduct of the future princes in comparison to the conduct of the former princes? (Ezekiel 45:9-12)

What do you learn about the responsibililties of the prince regarding offerings? (Ezekiel 45:13-17)

What do you learn about the responsibilities of the prince regarding the feasts? (Ezekiel 45:18-25)

A special privilege was made for the prince in Ezekiel 44:3. Note the specific location and what the privilege was.

Now carefully read the beginning of the next chapter, Ezekiel 46:1-3. Compare this to the location in Ezekiel 44:3.

What is being described?

Where is it located?

When is it used?

Who may use it?

Do you see that the Lord is ordaining a specific pattern of worship? In the past, the Israelites had broken the laws of the sanctuary. Priests had offered "profane fire" at the tabernacle in the wilderness when it was the duty of the High Priest alone. Kings entered the Most Holy Place when the Lord had appointed only the High Priest to do so. Gentiles had set up abominable idols on the "seat" of the Lord, where the ark of the covenant was located. The manner of worship prescribed in Ezekiel allowed for the temple to be treated as the Holy Place that it was. It was another opportunity for the people to keep the law of the temple, all of its ordinances, all of its forms, and all of its laws. Because the whole area is holy.

So far, in this grand vision of the future, since Ezekiel 40, we've studied the architectural plans, the people, the priests, the prince, and the places of worship. We've observed that the priests, the prince, and the people will present sacrifices and offerings to the Lord. Let's look more closely at these sacrifices now. Each of the offerings described in the Mosaic regulations are presented to the Lord during the Millennial reign.

Did the Old Testament sacrifices and offerings take away the sins of the people? Base your answer on Hebrews 10:1-4,10.

The offerings and sacrifices were to represent the people's heart of worship, but the people's hearts were as hard as stone. In the Millennial Kingdom, the Israelites will be able to worship the Lord with their new hearts; they will worship Him with all their heart, with all their soul, and with all their strength. Taking a literal interpretation of these Scriptures directs us to conclude that real sacrifices will be made. Keeping the whole Biblical context in mind leads us to understand these sacrifices as memorial ordinances, just as the Lord's Supper is a memorial ordinance for believers today.

I never knew how to worship until I knew how to love.[4]

HENRY WARD BEECHER (1813–1887)

Read Ezekiel 46:1-15. Look at the verses below, fill in the blanks and observe the parallels between the Millennial laws and the levitical laws.

The _____ offering in Ezekiel 46:13 and Leviticus 1:9b speaks of total dedication to the Lord.

The _____ offering in Ezekiel 42:13 and Leviticus 6:24-26 was brought by those who sinned through ignorance.

The _____ offering in Ezekiel 40:39 and Leviticus 7:1 dealt with offenses for which some kind of restitution should be made.

The _____ offering in Ezekiel 43:27 and Leviticus 7:11-12 was given to the Lord as an expression of praise and thanksgiving and occasion for worshipping the Lord and enjoyment with His people.

The _____ offering in Ezekiel 44:29-30 and Leviticus 2:1, 14-15 involved presenting sheaves, the roasted kernels of grain, fine flour, or various kinds of baked cakes. It was the acknowledgment that God is the source of the food that sustains life.

The _____ offering in Ezekiel 45:17 and Leviticus 23:13 was a portion of wine that was poured out along with another sacrifice. It symbolized life poured out wholly to the Lord. [5]

Not only will the worship of the Lord in the Millennial Kingdom involve sacrifices, but it will also involve some of the special feasts that were established after the exodus from Egypt. According to Ezekiel 45:17, the prince will be involved in presenting offerings during "the feasts, the New Moons, the Sabbaths, and at all the appointed seasons of the house of Israel."

The chart below describes the feasts and special occasions of the Israelites that are mentioned in the book of Ezekiel.

The Sabbath – Ezekiel 46:1,3 (Ex. 20:8-11; 31:12-17; Lev. 23:3; Deut. 5:12-	Every seventh day was a solemn rest from all work.
The New Moon – Ezekiel 46:1,3 (Num. 28:11-15; Psa. 81:3)	The first day of each month was a day of rest, special sacrifices, and the blowing of trumpets.
Passover – Ezekiel 45:21-24 (Ex. 12:1-14; Lev. 23:5; Num. 9:1-14; 28:16;	On the fourteenth day of the first month (Nisan), this festival commemorated God's deliverance of Israel from bondage in Egypt.
The Feast of Tabernacles (Booths or Ingathering) **– Ezekiel 45:25** (Ex. 23:16; 34:22; Lev. 23:33-36, 39-43; Num.	This eight-day celebration lasted from the fifteenth to the twenty-second day of the seventh month (Tishri).
The Year of Jubilee – Ezekiel 46:17 (Lev. 25:8-55; 27:17-24)	The fiftieth year, which followed seven Sabbath years, proclaimed liberty to those who were servants because of debt, and returned lands to their former owners.

We have now had an overview of the sacrifices and feasts that will be a part of the worship and celebration in the Millennial temple, prepared and enjoyed by the priests, the princes, and the people of Israel. Not only will the house of Israel bring offerings to the altar of the Lord, but others will as well.

What do you learn about worshippers and the temple from Isaiah's prophecy of the future kingdom?

Isaiah 56:6-8

Isaiah 60:1-7

Please finish our study of this section of Scripture by reading Ezekiel 46:1-25. You will be able to see the manner of worship as it was prescribed in its entirety.

When the Lord first showed Ezekiel a vision of the temple, before His judgment had been poured out upon Israel, the people, princes and priests were all guilty of heinous crimes committed in the temple. Their worship was false, idolatrous and impure. But the Lord had promised that He would give them a new heart so that they would walk in His statutes and keep His ordinances. They would enjoy new worship in spirit and in truth in the Millennial Kingdom.

Today, we as believers have the opportunity and privilege to worship the Lord with all of our hearts, but we must be cautious that we do not fall into hypocrisy or complacency.

What exhortation is given to believers regarding the ordinance of the Lord's Supper in 1 Corinthians 11:27-30?

What impact has our study today on worship in the Millennial Kingdom had on you?

DAY TWO   *The River of Life*   EZEKIEL 47:1-12

Pray for refreshment from the Word of the Lord today.

יהוה

After our intense studies of buildings, measurements, and ordinances, I'm ready to take a walk outside to see the softer side of the Lord's creation. And that's just what the Lord has planned for us in His Word today! I've been looking forward to this walk by the river. Please join me!

Read Ezekiel 47:1-12.

List everything that you observe about the water and the river.

I continue to enjoy how the Lord gives significance to every aspect of His Word. According to 1 Kings 7:23,39, Solomon placed at the south of the altar a massive bronze pool whose purpose was to provide water for cleansing. The river described in Ezekiel 47 flows from the south of the altar! And it certainly provides cleansing as it heals!

Look back at the description of how the river of life begins at the altar and flows out to the valley and the sea (which is the Dead Sea). Do you see anything out of the ordinary about this picture? How do rivers or streams normally begin? What happens to them as they travel through the land?

The Lord also gave visions of this river of life to His prophets Joel and Zechariah. Note the additional details that you learn from these passages.

Joel 3:18

Zechariah 14:4, 8

References to a life-giving river flow throughout the Scriptures. Enjoy them and note what you learn.

Genesis 2:9-14

Psalm 46:4-5

Isaiah 41:17-18

Revelation 22:1-2

I also find it very interesting that Ezekiel 47 is not the first time that "waters" have been mentioned in this book. In 48 chapters, "water" or "waters" are mentioned 40 times. I mentioned in an earlier lesson that the "land" is a very important aspect of the book of Ezekiel, so it's appropriate that "water" is running through the "land" in Ezekiel!

In his commentary on Ezekiel, Iain Duguid says, "the Gospel of John develops this vision of Ezekiel most fully." [7] You are probably already thinking of some familiar statements spoken by Jesus regarding living water. Let's look at what John wrote and find that the prophecy seen in Ezekiel's vision has been partially fulfilled.

Note what you learn about water, how it was used, what Jesus said about it, and where it came from.

John 4:13-14

John 7:37-39

John 13:5

Acts 1:4-5

Revelation 21:6

In the Old Testament and the New Testament the source of living water is _____.

What would we do without water? Our bodies are composed of over 70% water. It is essential for proper digestion and nutrient absorption. It is essential for proper circulation, and it helps remove wastes and toxins from our bodies. Water regulates our bodies' temperatures. Failure to drink enough water can lead to dehydration. We can apply these physical facts about water to our spiritual lives!

When Jesus spoke of Living Water, He was speaking of the Holy Spirit. We have no life without the Spirit. Remember the dry bones in Ezekiel 37? The bones came together and skin covered them, creating corpses – with "no breath in them." The Lord explained the demonstration in Ezekiel 37:14: "I will put My Spirit in you, and you shall live." Without the Spirit giving us understanding, we cannot digest and absorb the Word of God. Without the Holy Spirit controlling our lives, our temperatures can get pretty hot! Without the Holy Spirit, we are completely dehydrated and spiritually dead.

Are you thirsty? Take a drink from the following verses and note their truths:
Romans 8:11

Ephesians 1:13

You are sealed with the Spirit, but don't seal Him up in you. Let the fountain of living waters quench your soul and flow out through your words and actions that others around you might be refreshed and resuscitated.

Please enjoy taking another walk along the river of life. Read Ezekiel 47:1-12. Our literal interpretation of these Scriptures indicates that this river will flow in the land of Israel one day. The vision of the river in Israel is a continuation of the theme of abundant blessing, a garden of Eden paradisiacal setting, and a provision of food, fruit, and fish. All flows from the throne of God. He is the source of goodness and blessing.

Are you looking to Him today and trusting Him to cleanse, refresh and satisfy you?

Oh, Sweet River, flow through me
In an ever flowing fountain
In a never ending stream
Living Water, You are all I need
Oh, Sweet River, flow through me [8]

LESSON THREE   *The Covenant Fulfilled*   EZEKIEL 47:13-48:35

Our travel from the distant past to the distant future is almost complete. We have arrived at the last words of the book of Ezekiel. I pray that the Lord will encourage us and give us hope in Him just as He desired these words to do for His people in exile.

יהוה

If you have trusted in Jesus Christ as your Savior, then you are not in exile. You have been set free from the captivity of sin and death. You are, however, a stranger and an alien here on this earth. Your home is being prepared for you right now. We will see from our study in Ezekiel today that the Lord has quite some plans for the future home of His chosen people, the Israelites.

Please read Ezekiel 47:13-14.

This verse gives clear instructions for the rest of the passage. List the specific details spoken by the Lord.

How does the Word of the Lord in these verses relate to Genesis 17:7-8?

How does Ezekiel 47:13-14 compare to Numbers 34:13-15? What are the similarities and/or differences?

Before you read any further it will be helpful for you to look at a map! Locate the following landmarks and mark them with an asterisk.

    a. the Great Sea (the Mediterranean Sea)

    b. Zedad

    c. Hazar Enan

    d. Damascus

    e. Jordan River (draw a line)

    f. Tamar

    g. Meribah of Kadesh

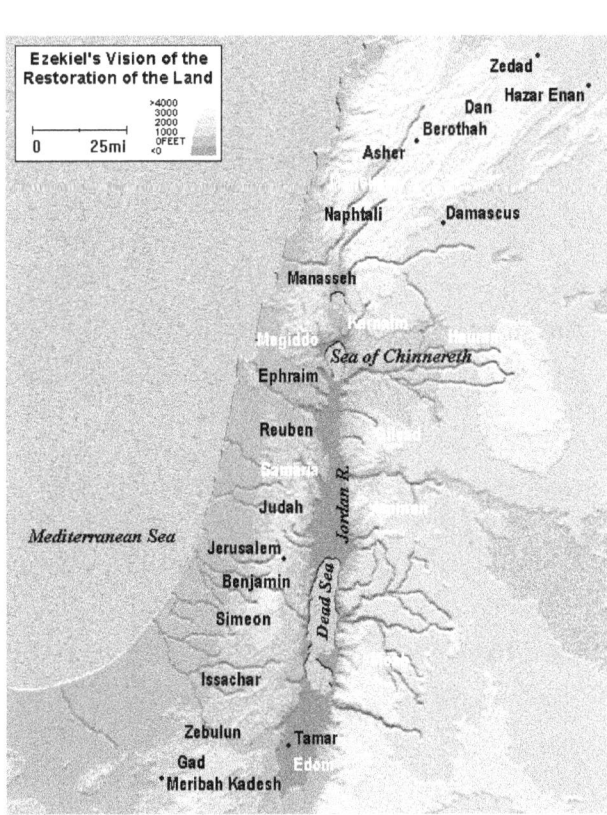

Now read Ezekiel 47:15-20, and then "connect the dots" to outline the future borders of Israel presented by the Lord.

247

Here's a map of the borders and divisions of the land after Joshua took the Israelites into the territory. And here's another map of the borders of Israel today. Neither look like the plan shown to Ezekiel! Does history or circumstance negate the Word of the Lord? You know it doesn't! One day, the map will look like the one described to Ezekiel.

Boundaries of Israel after Joshua[10]

Modern Boundaries of Israel[11]

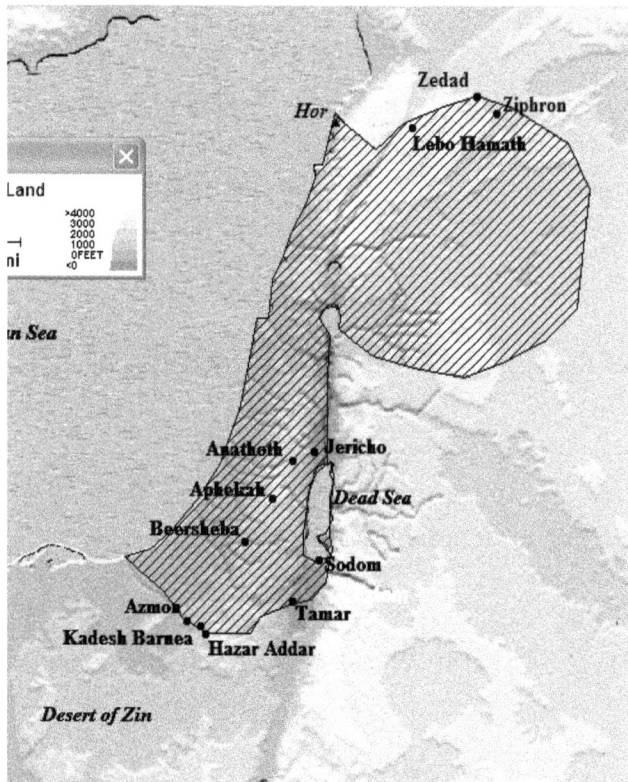

Is there any history in your life that causes you to doubt the promises of the Lord for you?

Are there any circumstances in your life today that make you think that it will be impossible for the Lord to carry out His purposes for you?

The Word of the Lord is true. Moses wasn't allowed to enter the Promised Land due to unbelief. Don't let unbelief steal your hope in the sure promises of the Lord for you.

Read Ezekiel 47:21-23 and note the specific instructions given by the Lord.

It is altogether unprecedented under the old covenant that "strangers" should have "inheritance" among the tribes.[12] *However, the desire of the Lord to gather His people together is seen throughout Scripture.*

Note what you learn from the following verses:

Leviticus 19:34

Romans 10:12

Ephesians 1:10

Ephesians 3:6

How does this truth impact your attitude toward different tribes, tongues, races, and nationalities today?

The lot is cast. And the Lord knows how it will fall. In Ezekiel 48, the Lord declares which tribe will inherit which section of land. Ezekiel 47:14 stated that the tribes would inherit their lands equally with each other. Most maps indicate the equal territories as shown below.

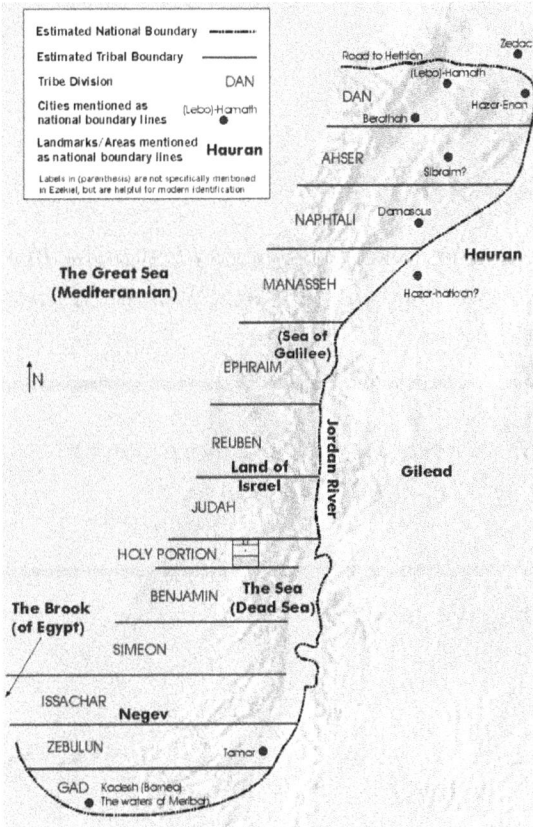

Read Ezekiel 48:1-7 and 23-29 and highlight the future inheritances of the twelve tribes of Israel on the map.[13]

And now we come to the last aspect of the vision given to Ezekiel, the district of the great city of God, the joy of the whole earth. In Ezekiel 48:8-35, there is a detailed layout given regarding the dwelling place of the Lord. We read a preliminary description in Ezekiel 45:1-8, and noticed that the most prominent feature of the district was that it is holy.

Slowly read Ezekiel 48:8-22, once again marking the word "holy" and then locate the holy district on the map. What is the land of the holy district used for?

The final details of the holy district given in Ezekiel are in reference to the city gates. We are ignorant of their importance to the Israelite communiy, so we need some historical background on them. To the ancient Israelites, the gates were a representation of the glory of the city. They were the first line of defense against enemy attack, therefore they had strong doors made of stone or wood plated with metal. The gates were the typically 13 to 14 feet wide and the center for the life of the city. Business was conducted in their open spaces whether it was selling goods and produce as a marketplace, or carrying on legal transactions. Large numbers of people would often be found at the city gates and they became a popular forum for teachers or prophets to give their messages. Even the kings held public audiences in them.

The Scriptures often mention the gates of the city, showing the importance that they played in the daily life of the ancient Israelites and at the time of Christ as well. The book of Nehemiah gives the most detailed description of the gates of Jerusalem, as Nehemiah surveyed the walls of Jerusalem after the return of the Jews from the Babylonian exile. Nehemiah lists the following gates, probably named according to how it was used, where it was located, or what was sold there.

    a. The sheep gate (Neh. 3:1).
    b. The fish gate (Neh. 3:3).
    c. The valley gate (Neh. 3:13).
    d. The dung gate (Neh. 3:14).
    e. The fountain gate (Neh. 3:15).
    f. The water gate (Neh. 3:26).
    g. The horse gate (Neh. 3:28).
    h. The east gate (Neh. 3:29).
    i. The Miphkad (meaning inspection or recruiting) gate (Neh. 3:31)

If I lived back then, if I weren't at the temple, I think I'd be at one of the gates! They sound like the place to meet and greet one another. Not the dung gate though! Now that we have a little background, let's read the Lord's plans for the future holy city's gates.

His foundation is in the holy mountains. The Lord loves the gates of Zion more than all the dwellings of Jacob. Glorious things are spoken of you, O city of God!
Psalm 87:1-3

Read Ezekiel 48:30-34 and list the details given regarding the gates.

Did you notice a difference in the listing of the tribes of Israel compared to the list of the tribes that inherit the equal sections of the land? What is the difference and why?

We've seen throughout our look at the millennial kingdom that the Lord's plans fulfill His promises spoken through Moses before the Israelites ever entered the Promised Land. What do you learn from Deuteronomy 31:10-13?

At the present time, there are eight gates in Jerusalem, but one has been sealed shut. The Eastern Gate in the wall around the city was permanenly closed by the Muslim Suleiman the Magnificent because he knew the Jews anticipated the return of the Messiah through the eastern gate. When Jesus Christ the Messiah comes back, no sealed gate will keep Him out of His holy city!

Please read Psalm 24:7-10 and note what it describes.

The King of Glory shall come in! Yes, He shall! When He arrives in the city, it will have a new name. Nowhere in the prophecy of Ezekiel 40 – 48 have we seen the city called Jerusalem or called by any other name. It is declared in the last sentence of the book of Ezekiel. It truly is the grand finale to the prophecy.

Please read it for yourself – Ezekiel 48:35 – and record the name of the city after the Lord returns to it.

This city will truly be the joy of the whole earth, for the Lord has chosen Zion; He has desired it for His dwelling place, saying "This is My resting place forever." (Psalm 131:13,14) Let the things you have seen and studied today soak in and lead you to worship your Lord, because He is there, with you, right now. We will continue rejoicing in all that He has done and all that He is going to do as we complete our final lesson in Ezekiel tomorrow.

LESSON FOUR — *The Lord Is There* — EZEKIEL 48:35

Today, I pray for you, that during this lesson you will encounter the presence of our living God. I pray that you may know the Lord as your holy and sovereign God, your wonderful Savior and Shepherd, and your life-giving, mind-enlightening Spirit.

יהוה

Please open your Bible to the last verse of the book of Ezekiel. We have come to the end, but can you tell that it is still just the beginning? Please record once again what you learn from this verse:

"And the name of the city from that day shall be _____."

YHWH SHAMMAH: The Lord is There. Not only is this the name of the city when the Lord returns, but it is one of the names of the Lord. He is our omnipresent God. He is there.

What do you learn about the presence of the Lord according to the following verses?
Psalm 139:7-13

Jeremiah 23:23-24

Can you escape the presence of the Lord? There once was a prophet who thought he would do just that! "Jonah arose to flee to Tarshish from the presence of the Lord." (Jon. 1:3) But Jonah experienced the presence of the Lord everywhere he went...in the storm at sea, in the belly of the whale, during the revival of Nineveh, under the shade of a tree, and in the scorching heat of the sun. If the Lord is always present everywhere, then why the special name for the city in the future? Remember the crucial moments that we have seen in this book: Ezekiel saw the glory of the Lord leave the temple because of the idolatry of the people. And then he saw the glory of the Lord return as the fulfillment of His covenant to be their God and dwell among them.

The Lord is present everywhere, but there is also a special manifestation of His shekinah glory which will return to Jerusalem "in that day." On that day the Israelites will say: "God with us! Hallelujah!" But, if you are in Christ, you don't have to wait until that day to rejoice in the presence of the Lord. God is with us now! Let's look at the Scriptures that show us the truth of this.

What do you learn about the presence of the Lord from the following verses? How is it manifested?

Matthew 1:23

John 14:18-20

Acts 18:9-10

2 Corinthians 13:14

2 Timothy 4:17

The Lord is here! The holy, awesome, sovereign God became a man and revealed Himself to us in person! And He, the God-Man, Jesus, made a new covenant available to anyone who would receive it. Through His blood poured out on the cross, we can receive a new heart with the laws of God written on it.

> *Jesus Christ came — that you may know the Lord.*
>
> *Jesus Christ came — that you may know that the Lord is here!*

On that incredible day in the future when the Lord returns to His temple in His glorious, tangible presence, the people will rejoice and declare that "The Lord is here!" Those who are not in the city will say "The Lord is there," but those in the city will know and experience the actual presence of the almighty God and say "He is here! The Lord is with us!"

How would you describe experiencing the presence of the Lord?

What attitudes and actions are described in the following Psalms regarding being in the presence of the Lord?

Psalm 16:11

Psalm 95:2

Psalm 100:2

There certainly will be times when we will not feel the presence of the Lord. This does not mean that He has left us. During these times, we must cling to the truth given to us in God's Word. Our faith may be tested to be strengthened, or we may go through a time of discipline requiring a change in our thoughts, beliefs, attitudes or actions.

Please look at the following verses and consider the truths they express.

Exodus 33:13-14

Matthew 28:20

Acts 3:19

The Israelites experienced the shekinah glory of the Lord, His very presence, during their exodus from Egypt. They experienced His presence as they conquered the land of Canaan, as they settled there, and as they grew as a nation under King David. They experienced His presence even as they committed atrocious idolatry against Him during the reign of the kings of Judah and the kings of Israel.

But then, the Lord left. The glory of the Lord departed from Jerusalem. And the word of the Lord came to Ezekiel. He experienced the presence of the Lord in all of His glory. He experienced the presence of the Lord in the power of the Spirit. He experienced the presence of the Lord as he received visions of the new covenant and the Shepherd-King.

יהוה

Please look back through this study, at the table of contents or your unit review pages. My prayer throughout this study has been that you may know the Lord… who He is, what He wants, how He acts, what His plans are for the future.

What is your favorite verse from the book of Ezekiel?

How have you experienced the presence of the Lord during your time in His Word? How have you come to know the Lord?

ENDNOTES

Week One—His Glorious Appearing
1. Edythe Draper, *Draper's Quotations for the Christian World*, Tyndale House Publishers, Inc. Wheaton, Illinois.
2. Chambers, Oswald, *My Utmost for His Highest*, Barbour Publishing Incorporated, 2003.
3. Penn-Lewis, Jesse, *Fruitful Living*, Christian Literature Crusade, Fort Washington, PA, 1992.

Week Two—The Ominous Warning
1. Draper, *Draper's Quotations.*
2. John Gill, *John Gill's Exposition of the Entire Bible*, www.e-sword.net
3. *Hard Sayings of the Bible*, Quickverse.
4. Draper, *Draper's Quotations.*

Week Three—Travesty in the Temple
1. Jamieson, Robert, A.R. Fausset, David Brown, *A commentary, critical and explanatory, on the whole Bible, with introduction to Old Testament literature, a pronouncing dictionary of Scripture proper names, tables of weights and measures, and an index to the entire Bible.* George H. Doran Co., New York, 1921.
2. Warren Wiersbe, *Be Reverent*, Cook Communications, Colorado Springs, CO, 2000.
3. David Augsberger, *Caring Enough to Confront*, Regal Books, Ventura, CA, 1981.
4. Draper, *Draper's Quotations.*

Week Four—The Truth is Told
1. J. Vernon McGee, *Ezekiel*, Thomas Nelson Publishers, Nashville, TN, 1991.
2. McGee, *Ezekiel.*
3. Wiersbe, *Be Reverent.*
4. Wiersbe, *Be Reverent.*
5. Keil, C F; F Delitzsch, *Keil and Delitzsch Commentary on the Old Testament*, www.e-sword.net
6. Clarke, Adam and Ralph Earl, *Adam Clarke's Commentary on the Bible*, Baker Book House, Grand Rapids, Michigan, 1967.

Week Five—Powerful Parables
1. Andrew Murray, *The True Vine*, Moody Press, Chicago, 1997.
2. Jamieson, Robert, A.R. Fausset, David Brown, *A commentary.*
3. Wiersbe, *Be Reverent*
4. Wiersbe, *Be Reverent.*

Week Six—Proclaiming the Prophecy
1. From *The Nelson Study Bible*, copyright © 1997 by Thomas Nelson, Inc. Used by permission.
2. From *The Nelson Study Bible.*
3. MacArthur, J. J. , *The MacArthur Study Bible* (electronic ed.), Word Publishing.: Nashville, TN, 1997.

Week Seven—The Refiner's Fire
1. Wiersbe, *Be Reverent.*
2. *Encyclopaedia Britannica*, Chicago, 2001.
3. Draper, *Draper's Quotations*
4. Passion, *Give Me One Pure and Holy Passion*, Sparrow Records.
5. Draper, *Draper's Quotations*
6. McGee, *Ezekiel.*
7. Keil, C F; F Delitzsch, *Keil and Delitzsch Commentary on the Old Testament.*

Week Eight—Foreign Policies
1. Strong, James, *The Strongest Strong's Exhaustive Concordance of the Bible*, Zondervan, Grand Rapids, Michigan, 2001.

2. Strong, James, *The Strongest Strong's Exhaustive Concordance of the Bible.*
3. Strong, James, *The Strongest Strong's Exhaustive Concordance of the Bible.*
4. Strong, James, *The Strongest Strong's Exhaustive Concordance of the Bible.*
5. From *The Nelson Study Bible.*
6. Bromily, Geoffrey William, *International Standard Bible Encyclopedia*, Eerdmans, Grand Rapids, Michigan, 1979.
7. Smith, William, *Smith's Bible Dictionary,* Hendrickson Publishers, Peabody, Massachusetts, 2002.
8. Bromily, Geoffrey William, *International Standard Bible Encyclopedia.*
9. Barnes, Albert, *Albert Barnes Notes on the Bible,* www.e-sword.net
10. M. G. Easton, *Easton's Bible Dictionary*, www.e-sword.net
11. Wiersbe, *Be Reverent.*
12. Wiersbe, *Be Reverent.*

Week Nine—A Change for the Better
1. Author Unknown
2. Coffman, James B., *James Burton Coffman Bible Study Library, Old Testament,* Abilene Christian University Press, 2001.
3. Gill, *Gill's Exposition*
4. Wiersbe, *Be Reverent.*

Week Ten—Medical and Military Operations
1. MacArthur Study Bible, Libronix Software
2. Adonai, Integrity Music, Word Records, 1998.
3. *Bible Knowledge Commentary*, Walvoord and Zuck, eds., Victor Books, 1989.
4. *Treasury of Scripture Knowledge*, e-sword.net
5. Piper, John, www.desiringgod.org.
6. Jamieson, Robert, A.R. Fausset, David Brown, *A commentary.*
7. Wiersbe, *Be Reverent.*
8. *Hard Sayings of the Bible*, Quickverse.

Week Eleven—Great Expectations
1. MacArthur, J. J., *The MacArthur Study Bible.*
2. Wiersbe, *Be Reverent.*
3. From *The Nelson Study Bible.*
4. From *The Nelson Study Bible.*
5. Jamieson, Robert, A.R. Fausset, David Brown, *A commentary.*
6. Wiersbe, *Be Reverent.*

Week Twelve—The Kingdom of Christ
1. MacArthur, J. J., *The MacArthur Study Bible.*
2. Ian Duguid, *The NIV Application Commentary: Ezekiel*, Zondervan, Grand Rapids, MI, 1999.
3. Wiersbe, *Be Reverent.*
4. Draper, *Draper's Quotations*
5. Wiersbe, *Be Reverent.*
6. Wiersbe, *Be Reverent.*
7. Duguid, *The NIV Application Commentary: Ezekiel.*
8. Living Proof Live, *Sweet River,* Genevox Music Group, Nashville, TN, 1998.
9. From *The Nelson Study Bible.*

SUGGESTED RESOURCES

Shepherd's Notes: Ezekiel. Paul P. Enns, editor ©1998, B&H Publishing Group, Nashville, TN.

The Strongest Strong's Exhaustive Concordance by James Strong — available through online resources below and Google

Suggested (free) online study helps:

These include various Bible translations and links to all resources mentioned below.

studylight.org   **searchgodsword.org**   **blueletterbible.org**

e-sword.net (free program to download, then available offline)

The following list includes study helps that are available for free online if you are interested in pursuing more information about the Scriptures on your own. Descriptions are from e-sword.net.

Commentaries:

Robertson's Word Pictures in the New Testament

Robertson's magnum opus has a reputation as one of the best New Testament word study sets. Providing verse-by-verse commentary, it stresses meaningful and pictorial nuances implicit in the Greek but often lost in translation. And for those who do not know Greek, exegetical material and interpretive insights are directly connected with studies in the original text. All Greek words are transliterated.

Treasury of Scriptural Knowledge

This classic Bible study help gives you a concordance, chain-reference system, topical Bible and commentary all in one! Turn to any Bible passage, and you'll find chapter synopses, key word cross-references, topical references, parallel passages and illustrative notes that show how the Bible comments on itself. This really is a treasure!

Vincent's Word Studies

Marvin Vincent's Word Studies has been treasured by generations of pastors and laypeople. Commenting on the meaning, derivation, and uses of significant Greek words and idioms, Vincent helps you incorporate the riches of the New Testament in your sermons or personal study without spending hours on tedious language work!

John Gill's Exposition of the Entire Bible

Having preached in the same church as C. H. Spurgeon, John Gill is little known, but his works contain gems of information found nowhere outside of the ancient Jewish writings. John Gill presents a verse-by-verse exposition of the entire Bible.

Jamieson, Fausset and Brown Commentary

Long considered one of the best conservative commentaries on the entire Bible, the JFB Bible Commentary offers practical insight from a reformed evangelical perspective. The comments are an insightful balance between learning and devotion, with an emphasis on allowing the text to speak for itself.

Keil & Delitzsch Commentary on the Old Testament

This commentary is a classic in conservative biblical scholarship! Beginning with the nature and format of the Old Testament, this evangelical commentary examines historical and literary aspects of the text, as well as grammatical and philological issues. Hebrew words and grammar are used, but usually in content, so you can follow the train of thought.

Dictionaries:

Easton's Bible Dictionary

Easton's Bible Dictionary provides informative explanations of histories, people and customs of the Bible. An excellent and readily understandable source of information for the student and layperson. This dictionary is one of Matthew George Easton's most significant literary achievements.

International Standard Bible Encyclopedia

This authoritative reference dictionary explains every significant word in the Bible and Apocrypha! Learn about archaeological discoveries, the language and literature of Bible lands, customs, family life, occupations, and the historical and religious environments of Bible people.

Smith's Bible Dictionary

A classic reference, this comprehensive Bible dictionary gives you thousands of easy-to-understand definitions, verse references and provides a wealth of basic background information that you'll find indispensable as you read the Bible.

Thayer's Greek Definitions

For over a century, Joseph Henry Thayer's Greek-English Lexicon of the New Testament has been lauded as one of the finest available! Based on the acclaimed German lexicon by C.L.W. Grimm, Thayer's work adds comprehensive extra-biblical citations and etymological information, expanded references to other works, increased analysis of textual variations, and discussion of New Testament synonyms. An invaluable resource for students of New Testament Greek!

Noah Webster's Dictionary of American English

Noah Webster once wrote, "Education is useless without the Bible." That's why his first dictionary is the only one available today that defines every word in the original language and its biblical usage. Compare Webster's definitions of words like "marriage" and "education" with those found in modern dictionaries, and see the difference for yourself.

OTHER STUDIES BY
ELIZABETH BAGWELL FICKEN

Immeasurably More!: An in-depth study of Ephesians

Do you want your walk with Christ to be more intimate, more faithful, and more obedient? God is able to do immeasurably more than you can imagine through His power in your life! This exciting study will help you understand the never-ending blessings of salvation and the extraordinary potential you have to live a victorious and faithful Christian life.

And the Lord Blessed Job: An in-depth study of Job

One of the Lord's blessings to Job was that he was chosen to show Satan that God is worthy of worship no matter what happens in our lives. While the book of Job deals with suffering, it isn't about answering the question "why do people suffer?" It's about humbly submitting to God as the Holy One who is infinite in wisdom, power, justice, and goodness.

Follow Me: An in-depth study of the Gospel of Matthew

This study will challenge you to a more passionate commitment to Jesus. Learn from Matthew's eye-witness perspective, his proofs from Old Testament scriptures, and his presentation of Jesus' five sermons, just who Jesus is, what He did, and what He said. Matthew's life was drastically changed from his encounter with Jesus—yours will be too.

Letters to the Thessalonians: An in-depth study of 1st and 2nd Thessalonians

These letters are about faith, hope and love; holiness, prayer, and perseverance; the will of God and the glorious return of Christ. And so much more! Almost every major doctrine of our faith is covered in these personal writings from the apostle Paul. Join me as we read someone else's mail. I'm sure you'll find a few things that you will think were written just to you!

Come Let Us Worship: An in-depth study of Psalms

The Psalms contain many of our most well-known Scriptures, offering comfort and expressing the emotions of our souls. They challenge us to godly living, always trusting the Lord. What a beautiful arrangement of poems, prayers, and praises God has given us! From Psalm 1 to Psalm 150, you'll study selected psalms in the order of their placement in the Scriptures.

Find her! elizabethficken.com or

Available at
amazon.com
and other bookstores